Narcissistic Abuse Healing Guide

Follow the Ultimate Narcissists Recovery Guide, Heal and Move on from an Emotional Abusive Relationship! Recover from Narcissism or Narcissist Personality Disorder!

By Victoria Hoffman

Contents

TABLE OF CONTENT
INTRODUCTION

CHAPTER 1 - SUCCESS STORIES

Introduction to Narcissistic Characters
Success Stories of Narcissistic Abuse
Case Study #1: Lilie's Experience with a Narcissistic Husband
Case Study #2: Kelly Detaches Herself from Her Narcissistic Family

CHAPTER 2 - VICTIM MODE

What Makes It Hard to Heal from A Narcissistic Abuse
The Clarity in Retrospect
Learned powerlessness
The Lonely Road
Fear of the Unknown
Laying Down the Facts
Don't Expect Them to Change.
The Cornerstone of Healing
Ask Why
Be Specific

BE KIND TO YOURSELF

Be Smart
Stay on Top

CHAPTER 3 - GETTING RID OF THE PSEUDO PERSONALITY

How to Acknowledge Your Pseudo Personality
The Challenges of Dealing with a Pseudo Personality
Understanding Their Fragile Ego Could Be a Major Challenge
Comprehending Their Ability to Shift Gears from the Real to the False World
The Pseudo Personality Is Pretty Controlling
It May Be Challenging to Identify the Nitty-Gritty of a Pseudo Personality
A Pseudo Personality Is a Professional Liar
It May Be Difficult to Deal with Their Vicious Temper
The Pseudo Personality Will Always Play a Victim
Breaking the Machination

CHAPTER 4 - INNER CHILD HEALING

How Does It Happen?
The Inner Child in Adulthood
What Does a Stable Childhood Look Like?
Caring for Your Inner Child
Identifying Childhood Pain
Re-Parenting Your Inner Child
Engaging Your Inner Child

CHAPTER 5 - CREATING YOUR THOUGHTS

Awareness
Hearing of the Inner Voice
Negative and positive thinking
5 Steps to Regain Control of Your Thoughts
Get Rid of The Poor Self-Concept of Your Thoughts
Live in the Moment

CREATE AWARENESS
INSCRIBE IN A JOURNAL
DON'T JUDGE
BE CONNECTED TO YOURSELF
ENHANCE WATCHFUL MEDITATION
HAVE PARTICIPATION IN YOUR PERSONAL LIFE
ADVANCED BEGINNER'S MIND
LET GO
HAVE COMPASSION TO YOURSELF
REFOCUS YOUR MIND
BEGIN BY ASSESSING YOUR MENTAL FOCUS
ERADICATE INTERFERENCES
PUT YOUR FOCUS ON ONE THING AT A TIME
BE IN THE MOMENT
EXERCISE MINDFULNESS
TAKE A SMALL BREAK
PRACTICE MORE TO STRENGTHEN YOUR FOCUS
TIPS FOR IMPROVING MINDFULNESS
HOW TO AFFIRM YOURSELF

CHAPTER 6 - SURVIVAL MODE

IS IT PTSD?
HOW CAN YOU TELL IF YOU HAVE C-PTSD?
INTRUSIVE DEPRESSING THOUGHTS
STRESS
AVOIDANCE
EXCLUSION
CHANGES IN AROUSAL AND REACTIVITY
DIFFICULTY CONTROLLING EMOTIONS
ALTERED PERCEPTION OF SELF AND WORLD

- Obsession with the Abuser
- Difficulty with Personal Relationships
- Getting Help
- Finding a Support Group
- Identify Early Warning Triggers
- Identify Coping Methods
- Psychotherapy
- Cognitive-Behavioral Therapy
- Medications
- Gratitude Exercises
- Appreciate Yourself
- Keep a Gratitude Journal
- Schedule a Gratitude Visit
- Make a Gratitude Jar
- Laugh Out Loud
- Make a Daily Goal
- Find a Gratitude Buddy
- Reduce Your Complaints
- Act of Kindness
- Gratitude Prompts
- Make a Collage

CHAPTER 7 - THRIVING MODE

- Set Boundaries
- Be Assertive
- Know Your Rights
- Be Strategic
- Check for Abuse
- Check Your Silence
- Check Your Anger

Check for Their Willingness to Change
Be Aware of Manipulation
Honesty to Yourself
Be Educated
Confront Abuse Effectively
Have Consequences
Get Support and Purpose Elsewhere
Trust Your Intuition

CHAPTER 8- GETTING INTO A NEW RELATIONSHIP

Signs You Are Ready for a New Relationship
You Don't Think About Them Anymore
You Have No Hatred for Them
When You Can Open up Freely
You Don't Stalk Them Anymore
You Don't Feel Wrong About Your past Experiences
You Have No Fear of Falling for a Similar Person Again
You Take Care of Yourself
You Are Ready to Take the Risk Again
You Genuinely Want to Start a New Relationship
Redefining Sexy After a Narcissistic Relationship
Don't Think You Are Unattractive; Make Yourself Attractive Instead
Don't Let Your Past Relationship Affect Your Current Life
Find Your Confidence
Dress Well and Give Yourself a Treat
Maintain the Right Posture
Learn the Skills of a Good Romance
Love Yourself and Your Life
How to Become Your Own Source of Happiness

Make Yourself a Priority
Do the Little Things You Love More Often
Challenge Yourself by Doing Something New
Get Enough Sleep
Do the Workouts
How to Stay Single and Blessed
Learn to Do Things on Your Own
Develop Other Relationships
Meet New People
Maintain a Supportive, Positive Company

CONCLUSION

Introduction

Congratulations on purchasing Narcissistic Abuse Healing Guide. In society today, we get to interact with people with different personalities in many areas, including work, school, and relationships. Unfortunately, some of us have interacted with unhappy and disappointed people who lack self-esteem and lack empathy for others; these people are the so-called narcissists. Victims of narcissism may suffer from anxiety, stress, and depression, which can also contribute to other health problems.

Deciding to embark on the healing journey through this book, you have taken the first step towards learning how to get away and recover from narcissistic abuse. The information that you find in the following chapters is critical as it will guide you to take control of your life and develop a healthier mind and personality.

This book provides an in-depth view of narcissistic personality disorder, giving a clear understanding of the character traits of narcissists, success stories of narcissistic abuse recovery, and the healing process. It also covers the narcissistic victim mode, unraveling the circumstances surrounding the victim, the foundations needed to heal, and the challenges faced to recover from the abuse.

The book also offers a comprehensive account of the pseudo personality and how to get rid of it, proposing the strategies necessary for dealing with pseudo personality, including the possible challenges and how to acknowledge that you have a pseudo personality.

Chapter 1 - Success Stories

To give love, we must love ourselves first. This statement appears to be true that most of us fail to examine it thoroughly. In day-to-day affairs, be it business, love, or in the family setup, we act on this premise, yet it is questionable.

While some people believe that they do not love themselves at all (ego-dystonic group), others feel they have self-love because they are contented by who they are (ego-syntonic). Yet other people restrict their definition of love concerning their traits, behavioral patterns, and personal history. But there appears a group of people with a unique mental constitution – the narcissists.

Introduction to Narcissistic Characters

The belief is that Narcissists are in love with themselves. However, this is not the case. A narcissist is always in love with his REFLECTION rather than being in love with HIMSELF.

Being in love with oneself is functional, healthy, and adaptive, but having a love for your self-reflection is associated with two setbacks: the person continuously depends on the availability of the reflection to develop self-love and the lack of "an objective and realistic yardstick" as to whether the reflection exists in reality.

A common misconception is that narcissists always love themselves. But in reality, their love is always directed at other people's approval of them. A person whose love is formed on an impression cannot genuinely love other people, including himself.

A narcissist has a desire to feel loved and to love others, which means that if he is unable to love himself and others, he must be in love with his reflection amidst the possible contrast with his self-image. Unlike an ordinary person, a narcissist would invest a lot of energy and other resources to maintain the projected image, sometimes becoming vulnerable to external threats.

But a significant trait that projects the image of a narcissist is lovability. A narcissist will always associate love with other emotions like respect, attention, awe, and admiration. Thus, for a narcissist, a projected image is usually loveable and can be loved, thus, equating it to self-love. This character drains narcissists of their mental energy, thereby lacking any energy to dedicate to other people.

Success Stories of Narcissistic Abuse

I developed an interest in understanding narcissism in 2014 when I had the opportunity to visit a 3-day Narcissistic Abuse Recovery Program held in Brooklyn. During the event, I met several survivors of narcissistic abuse as well as those who still were trapped with narcissists. But the most intriguing story was that involving three subjects, Lilie, who had separated from her narcissistic husband, Joe, and Kelly, who escaped from his narcissistic family members. In this section, I will share their experience with narcissists and how they recovered from the abuse.

Case Study #1: Lilie's Experience with a Narcissistic Husband

When Lilie stood before the congregation, she began to sob even before uttering a word. She seemed to have put the matters behind her, but still, the wound seemed fresh. She had just walked out of her 12 years marriage and had taken her two children to live with her mother. She said she had been blinded for more than ten years not to recognize that she was living with a narcissist. When she began talking, I felt a personal connection with her pain; she started to tell of how she met her husband back in her college days,
"I remember how we met back in college, at the beginning of the summer. I had just joined campus, and the person who was ready to give me orientation was Josh, who was already a second year. That

day he showed me everywhere, including the classes, the laboratories, the botanical areas, and eventually to his room, where he happily welcomed me. By the end of the day, I knew I had met a friend, and as history would have it, we soon began dating."

Lilie explained how they were always together, and Josh would take her everywhere as long as he was free. After three years of dating, Josh took her to meet his parents in the summer holidays, who seemed very nice people. However, she recalled observing her boyfriend being too controlling with his parents during her stay there, something she had never felt (or too ignorant to notice). He would dictate what is to be cooked, how he would be treated, and the help he would render to his family. When she asked about the negative attitude, he told her, "you don't know how mean these people are. Just shut up."

After they graduated, they decided to get married. Although the wedding was fabulous, Lilie recalled that Josh changed after they were married. He would no longer let her go out to meet her friends, telling her that she needed more time to concentrate on her newly built home. He would accompany her to the groceries and any other places she wanted to go to during the weekends, and on weekdays, he would frequently check on her without notice.

"At first, I thought that Josh just wanted to spend time with me, but I came to realize later that he was a narcissist. When he found me talking to my male colleagues, he would intentionally engage me in a heated argument about not being dedicated to our marriage and flirting with men. He would even call me names like whore or sl**t then later apologize."

Lilie began to blame herself, feeling that she never loved Joe enough. She, therefore, resorted to not having any conversation or social engagement with her male colleagues except with her bosses. She would later abandon all her female friends and sisters since she believed they were a waste of time and did not add value to the marriage. But things got even worse when she had her first-born".

"When I had my first baby, I had gained a lot of weight. Joe considered that a weak point and would mock me about it. He was never there for any of us, and I was left struggling alone. He was distant emotionally and sexually, and one time he told me that he lost interest in me because I was fat."

Lilie spoke further about how she plunged into depression and recalled falling sick often because of stress. Joe would tell her that he preferred other women because she was no longer good enough, but she endured all the traumatizing abuse to keep her marriage going. She soon had her second baby after three years, and the state of her marriage grew even worse.

"After our second baby, Joe wanted me to leave my career so that I can babysit. He believed he had enough money to take care of us, so I didn't have a reason to work. But I still did not lose myself to that extent. I love my art job, and I wouldn't have sacrificed it at all. When I refused, my husband became violent; he associated my going to work with me having an opportunity to meet men. I would cry throughout the night as he would abuse me before the children. But my childrens' nanny opened my eyes."

Lilie learned that her nanny had experienced a similar married life before she decided to get divorced. Unfortunately for her (nanny), she never had a good career to move onto. She was abused for a long time, but when the beatings were too much, she decided to go and look for casual jobs. When Lilie heard her story, it became an eye-opener to her. She realized that she was living with a narcissist who had psychological issues.

She, therefore, decided to record her husband during an argument one evening. She then took the recording to court, where she filed a divorce and children's lawsuit. Eventually, she got her freedom and swore not to have such an ugly experience again.

Case Study #2: Kelly Detaches Herself from Her Narcissistic Family

"The moment I knew I had to part ways with my narcissistic family is when my father died," Kelly spoke about her experience sorrowfully that many people in the group shed tears. She recalls how she had been so close to her father. Being the first-born child in the family, her parents held high expectations for her and wanted her to get a better education to take care of her three other siblings later.

But their dream was halted when her father was diagnosed with cancer. He had been the breadwinner of his family; he was a dedicated banker and a part-time businessman. When he got sick, Kelly's mother took over the business, which she ran with her other sisters, who were 23 and 25, respectively. Because of financial strains, ranging from hospital bills, house bills, and the education costs of her younger siblings, Kelly was forced to drop out of her postgraduate nursing course and look for an internship at a local hospital. She made every effort to contribute as much money to the family budget, but her mother did not appreciate her efforts.

"I worked both day and night because I wanted my father to get the best medication. Since his former employer did not cover him for chronic diseases, he had to resign and use whatever we generated for his hospital bills. But my mom was never there for him at all. I felt that the business was doing well and that she could support my father's treatment with no strain."

Kelly describes how her mother stopped taking care of the father, telling her constantly that she and her children needed the money more because they have more days to live. The most painful moment that Kelly remembers is how her mother repeatedly abused the dad for choosing a poor lifestyle,
"She blamed my dad's poor habit and excess alcohol intake for being the cause of his cancer. She even told him that he was better off dead than continue draining the little money available."

Although Kelly ensured she took care of her father, she became depressed because of the mistreatment she saw from the other members of the family. Her other siblings never bothered to offer emotional support to the dad and would never accompany him to the hospital. They always blamed my dad for being sick and blamed me for neglecting them by focusing all my attention on my dad.
Due to the torture that his father received, he ended his life by overdosing on the prescribed cancer drugs,

"I remember that night vividly. I had taken my dad home before I went back to work in the afternoon. And when I returned home, I found the house so quiet. When I went to his room, he was lying there helplessly, with bottles of drugs scattered on the floor. But he had no pulse."

Kelly believes that her family members were not only sadists but also narcissists because of their self-centeredness. When the dad was alive, he took care of their mom and all of the siblings. However, when he got sick, everyone turned against him and blamed him for his chronic diseases instead of offering support.

Once her dad was buried, Kelly decided to separate herself from the family and live in a different city. She wished things were different, but she has not been able to forgive any of them.

Chapter 2 – Victim Mode

Living a life of manipulation, violation, and being lied to can have severe consequences to you as the victim. Healing from the damage the narcissist has left in you can be difficult, primarily if you blame yourself. You may ask how you could have possibly let that kind of person in your life — someone who caused you so much pain. However, you can break the chains of manipulation and be free from them (if you still are), and heal from the damage they have caused you.

What Makes It Hard to Heal from A Narcissistic Abuse

The disparity of truth: Why is it hard to recover from the damage the narcissist has caused? Why is it so hard to get over it? It is humans' natural need to have a connection with others. To be cared for and also to give love. When others hurt you, the pain won't matter because you have that one person who truly cares about you. But what happens when pain is from the one you care about? Usually, you might walk away from the pain and the person, no matter how much you care for them. But with a narcissist, things are different.

A narcissist will initially shower you with passionate love and attention; this is called love bombing. He studied you and all your trigger points. What you liked most and what you were your insecurities. He will then use that to his advantage; flatter and reassure you. It will feel good at first until it doesn't. Narcissist uses love bombing as a tool to build themselves to you as the perfect lover or friend. They intend to win you over to control you.

The thing with a narcissist relationship is that it is difficult to comprehend what is happening to you. You will get addicted to his "love," and you will find yourself constantly seeking his attention, craving for his approval. Once you are under his control, you will notice the hurting comments here and there. You will brush it off, thinking it's a mistake. With time, you will see that the behavior seems off, and so you will blame yourself.

The Clarity in Retrospect

You can spot the signs; how he treats you, how he manipulates you. You know that you deserve better. But when it comes to letting go, you think you will not survive without them. Your friends and family will even wonder why you are with such a person. However, you might find it difficult to answer because you have no valid answer.

According to psychologists, most victims of narcissists don't even know that they are in an abusive relationship. This explains why most of them stick around. People associate abuse with physical. You should understand that manipulation, gaslighting, and all forms of psychological and emotional abuse are part of violence.

According to Dr. Craig Malkin, the author of Rethinking Narcissism, the narcissist will find a way back into your life even though you might not want them. Narcissists are battling with themselves about whether to push you away or have you in their lives. For this reason, when you break off the relationship, they will find a way back. They don't leave without a fight.

You will keep letting them back in because your mind and heart are not on the same page. Your heart says you care about this person, while your mind says they are toxic, and you should let them go. This lack of agreement may go on for months or even years without being resolved.

Learned powerlessness

Picture this situation. You are in the middle of the ocean, a thousand miles away from civilization, when a tragedy happens. Your boat experiences an engine problem that you can't fix. You didn't carry a phone or something that could call for help. So what do you do? Nothing. Maybe sit and wait for a miracle.

Being in a narcissistic relationship is similar to being in a damaged boat in the middle of the ocean. You feel powerless because you are not in control.

Powerlessness doesn't occur abruptly in a toxic relationship, and you will be subject to abusive situations. Regular insults, manipulations, and gaslighting will eventually make you feel you have no control over what is happening in your life. Over time, you will feel immobilized. You will feel unable to take care of your own needs, even those that seem simple. A narcissist will abuse you until the powerlessness becomes internalized.
Healing will be difficult when you feel powerless. You will feel you don't deserve to be happy or free from abuse.
Learned powerlessness will also make you helpless. You will be unable to speak up or seek help from those who can offer assistance. You will also be unable to trust people because of the pain and damage you experienced.

In most cases, a victim of an abusive relationship will end up in another toxic relationship if they do not heal. You will be attracted to people who have similar traits to your ex because you feel you don't deserve better.

The Lonely Road

A victim of a narcissistic relationship will find it hard to heal because of the lonely journey. Loneliness will start pretty early in the relationship. Your lover will isolate you from your friends and family and make you believe you are alone.

Love and attention might have driven you into the arms of an abusive partner, but lack of control might be the glue that kept you there.

A narcissistic partner who made you believe that you couldn't possibly survive without them will exert total control over your life, that you feel helpless without them. His efforts would go into making you believe that life out there is difficult. Of course, this is not true unless you don't get a supportive system.

If your efforts to reach out for help go unanswered, you will get accustomed to living independently. You will slowly realize that things will always be hard for you. That no matter what you do, you are on your own.

When your family tries to help but cannot understand your situation, it will only frustrate you leading to you pull away. You will find yourself tolerating the pain for far too long. Victims of narcissists end up on a lonely journey of pain and shame over what they have experienced.

Fear of the Unknown

Even though the most logical thing to do would be to walk away from a toxic relationship, fear of the unknown will hold you back. Irrespective of how unhappy you are, your distrust of the world will make you stay in the relationship.

Fear of the unknown will keep you from healing from the harm caused by your narcissist lover. Just like loneliness, your partner will make you believe life without them is difficult. You will be conditioned to think there is nothing better for you out there.

Fear of the unknown will also make you not envision a better future for yourself. When other people expect serenity and peaceful existence for themselves, in your case, these thoughts will be so foreign. Through your partner's behavior, you will be convinced that there is nothing better for you. That the future is blank and every step you take towards it is doomed.

Trapped in fear, you will dismiss any hope of support systems available out there. You won't even consider whether other people are experiencing the same thing. When walking around, you may see happy people on the streets, but the thought that you could also be happy won't cross your mind.

A victim of a narcissistic relationship will get accustomed to the abuse until they believe that it is how the world is. You will tell yourself it's better to stay in a place where you are familiar, unlike the unknown. If you had a previous toxic relationship, you would resign on the thought of leaving. According to you, the world is the same.

Fear of the unknown will prevent you from forming healthy relationships and end up living in isolation.

Laying Down the Facts

You may wonder why a person would choose to stay in a place that is not conducive to them. Or why someone would want to hold onto pain. The thing is, when you are exposed to abuse over a long time, leaving becomes difficult.

Victims may hold on to pain or stay in a toxic relationship for various reasons — fear of leaving, for the sake of children, and the idea that the partner will change. But the truth is, holding onto pain for whatever reason is not doing yourself justice.

The narcissist in your life planned everything from the word go. After he studied and knew all your weak points, he hatched a plan to win you over. You ended up hooked to his "love." He needed you to be what he is. You were his target audience.

A narcissist needs an audience. So, they will cultivate relationships quickly with anyone who pays to listen. As their façade starts to slip up and their reality sets in, they will try to hide their shortcomings. They fear that people will see their flaws in the person they are.

The narcissist has an inflated sense of self. Everything they do revolves around them. They will do everything at the expense of others. According to Jacklyn Krol, a psychotherapist and a licensed clinical social worker, narcissists talk about their accomplishments and successes with grandiose. They will also exaggerate what they have achieved to impress their audiences.

As a victim, when you finally choose to see through his façade, you will realize how shallow they are. You will notice how all the conversations you had were centered on them and their lives.

He noted how empathetic you were and choose you as his target. Most people with a narcissist personality disorder have low self-esteem, according to Shirin Peykar, a Licensed Marriage and Family therapist.

Don't Expect Them to Change.

The truth is people don't break easily; they only change when they want to. He is never going to be the person you wish him to be. Often, you may find yourself reminiscing of the past moments where he was sweet and loving. However, you should remember that it was all a game—a plan to win you over.

A narcissist only thinks of himself. Whatever he does is centered on his needs. You may hold onto hope, thinking he will change. You may wonder why he changed for the worst and not for the better. But something you should remember is that even though change is possible, someone has to want it.

Understand that you deserve happiness, and expecting them to change won't help you in any way.

Most of the time, the narcissist will promise to change; this will give you hope for a while until it doesn't happen. Without any effort to change or seek help, his promises to change will be a way to seek control over you.

If he chooses to change, he will have to go through this process:

- He should understand that his actions are causing harm to you
- He should also despise the behavior so much he wants to let it go
- When making a negative choice unknowingly, he should immediately recant it and make a better one.
- He should also know that he has a choice in every situation, including how he treats those around him.

According to Jacklyn, you were never the problem: Victims will blame themselves for their partner's behavior in a narcissistic relationship. You will say to yourself, "he was good when we met and during our first dates. So, I must have done something that made him change." But this is not right.

People with narcissist personality disorder don't care about other people's feelings in any way. So quit blaming yourself for his behavior. You were never a problem.

Narcissists exhibit a grandiose image of themselves. They think they only matter and should only be associated with people of a higher class than them. Narcissists seek admiration from those around them, which is why they will exaggerate their achievements and accomplishments.

Narcissistic personality disorder might be born or acquired. Usually, this happens during childhood. If the parents or guardians were critically harsh towards him, that could be the cause. Heinz Kohut, a psychoanalyst in a study on his clients, observed the following: Narcissists went through a life of alienation, helplessness, and emptiness. They lacked the structures to form stable and meaningful relationships and a positive self-perception.

When they have a negative image of themselves, shame sets in, taking it out on others. They degrade others to feel good about themselves. They project their insecurities through the manipulation of others, especially those close to them. For the victims that are not aware of this, they end up blaming themselves.

You shouldn't feel sorry for them: For an empathetic person, it is reasonable to feel sorry for people around you, including your narcissist lover/friend. However, you should remember that people with narcissist personality disorder suffered an emotional injury from an early age. For this reason, they are incapable of feeling sorry for anyone but themselves. You may not believe that the person who showed you kindness and sympathy would turn out to be a narcissist.

A lot of times, victims of a narcissist will try to apologize for their wrongdoings. Usually, this happens when they notice your attempts to leave them. They will plead with you not to leave them.

A narcissist will use manipulation to have their way with the target audience and avoid any accountability. Once you understand how a narcissist's mind works, you will not feel sorry for his actions.

The narcissist knows what they are doing: The reality is that every person has a bit of narcissism. But for the narcissist, they score higher than the rest of us. Their move is carefully planned and executed.

Every person makes a mistake, and what differentiates a narcissist from the rest is the unwillingness to take charge of their choices. Typically, when a person makes a mistake, they take responsibility and humbly apologize for it. However, the narcissist doesn't even say sorry when they wrong you. He will choose to offer a fake apology to get on the right side with you.

But the real question is, does he change after the apology? The truth is, when a narcissist apologizes, he does so for himself and not because he cares about your feelings.

According to the author of Healing from Hidden Abuse, Shannon Thomas, emotional and psychological abusers know what they are doing. They know the right buttons to press. They know when to turn off their manipulative tendencies. They know what to do to get a response from their victims — showing that they are intelligent beings — people who know what they are doing.

The Cornerstone of Healing

Understand that it is possible to heal. Most victims of a narcissistic relationship find it hard to recover because of the damage to their self-esteem. As mentioned earlier, healing is possible. Here is what you should do first:

Ask Why

Asking yourself why this happened to you will open up many doorways into things you have never known. For instance, why you were his target. When you ask these questions, you will get many insights that will help prevent a similar situation in the future. Similarly, it will create a chance for you to choose to heal.

When you understand why you were the target, you will find ways to strengthen your weaknesses. So that in the future, you can see through a person's fakeness.

Be Specific

When you look into why you were the victim, it is wise to determine what made you the target accurately. Is it you empathetic. Were you desperate for love and attention? Narcissists study their victims first before making a move. So, it is best to know what exactly triggered him to you.

Be Kind to Yourself

It's important not to blame yourself because of the actions of the abusers. You will find it easier to heal and let go when you understand that some things are beyond your control.

Narcissist actions are solely based on his desires; even though he chooses you as his victim, understand it has nothing to do with you.

Be Smart

When healing happens, you will be more careful about the kind of people you let close to you. You will no longer entertain love bombing from a love interest. You can choose to walk away when the relationship shows signs of any manipulation. It means you can tell a person to back off when everything is about them.

Being smart in the decisions you make will help you in a great way. Besides healing, you will be able to understand a lot about different human personalities. It is essential to deal with past hurts and forgive yourself so that you can move forward.

Stay on Top

No man is an island. Go out and meet new people. You can seek the help of support groups, which will help you in the recovery journey. Just like any other problem, yours has a solution, and healing is part of it.

You can also choose to be a role model to others going through a similar situation. This usually happens when you trust that you have dealt with all the hurtful things.

You will also notice that when helping others, you will be able to heal all the wounds because, in a support group, people will look up to you and give you respect, which you didn't get in the relationship with the narcissist. You will see that it is possible to be loved and respected.

As shown in this chapter, many things can make it hard for victims to deal with the narcissist in their lives. However, it is also possible for them to heal from the abuse.

Chapter 3 - Getting Rid of The Pseudo Personality

The term pseudo personality refers to falsehood or pretense. Therefore, the psychology of pseudo personality is highly appended to the practice of deception. It is also best thought of as one that dominates a pre-cult personality. As such, it's not to be confused with multiple different personalities. To some extent, it's a clone of the leader of the same ideas, beliefs, values, and even behaviors, meaning that a pseudo is also an individual who fakes many things. For instance, it could be an intellectual attempting to convince someone else that they have a great educated mind, although they may not possess such greatness. A pseudo-celebrity may be an infamous individual thinking that they are prominent for doing something. In the real sense, they may not be as famous. But, having understood the traits of a pseudo personality, how can an individual get rid of this personality? How can a person tell if they have a pseudo personality?

How to Acknowledge Your Pseudo Personality

This chapter investigates the possible explanations for the extensive development of the pseudo personality, also known as a cult. We also dig deep into how the personality forms. We investigate the doubling of the pseudo personality, its adaptation, and dissociation. We argue that this is one of the most proposed concepts of introjections. Briefly, we discuss various recovery issues regarding the proposed view of the cult-centered personality. Towards that end, we also address what it takes to acknowledge your pseudo personality. When a person is born into a high-controlling family by nature, it enforces a significant separation from the ways of the world. Therefore, the individual develops a pseudo personality from a young age. In many cases, they are subject to different expectations and demands utilized in creating submissions coupled with conformity.

Apart from that, a person with a pseudo personality is exposed mainly to two different world forms. For instance, they live in the real world. But they may also be attached to the insular cultic world. This is especially common among people who have attended a public school. The two worlds, which are distinct from each other, carry various yet unique values and beliefs. It is vital to know the valid system so that you're not left confused or conflicted in any way. You will have to make a decision based on which world is safer for you. You will also need to identify key conditions that can make your life easier. You will realize that no world is safe in isolation. At the same time, being a young individual subjected to the world of pseudo personality, you'll encounter different symptoms of depression and anxiety. The intense pressure appended to thinking as well as acting in two significant ways introduces the cult identity.

The pseudo personality represses a person's original self while dissociating the defensive element in an individual. Therefore, it often allows the mind to cope with easily and then adapt to the intense demands of a group of environment. Critical thinking, questions, in addition to feelings, are squashed. In a way, the person becomes selfish and disloyal, thereby entering into a certain feeling of indifference. Over the years, toxic shame becomes the norm. Dependency coupled with insecurity will then become another aspect appended to this personality disorder. It's created at a young age as a person is growing.

For this reason, you treat the world as your enemy. Your true self then becomes stifled to receive some form of acceptance from the community. You'll also seek love and compassion from your family, meaning that your perception of yourself is destroyed. Shame takes over your personality.

In puberty, you become guiltier of actions that you may not be responsible for. After that, you would begin to lose friends and your immediate extended family. At some point in your life, you will realize that the risk of being a closed bud is more painful and disturbing than that of blossoming. When you reach your thirties, you'll delve into self-destruction. The people controlling you will make sure that this occurs.

In addition, children raised in different religious cults may be subjected to high expectations by the ministers and parents to submit to various group teachings. They will also be subjected to intense pressure based on thinking and acting in two different ways that cause a cult identity. That is how the pseudo or cult personality starts to form. It represses its original self in different ways. It also dissociates the mind in coping with the contradictory, intense demands of a particular environment. As an adult, when you associate with a totalitarian group that you did not spend your younger life with, you will be encouraged to reconnect to your older self before joining the destructive life. Unfortunately, toddlers who have grown in an oppressive environment encounter difficulties with the pseudo personality since the child's true self and critical thinking skills are hindered from developing.

A child raised in a harsh structure has to learn to live according to two different sets of rules: the world overview and the cult's teachings. Every element described in these worlds has some unique aspects. They both carry different values and teachings too. For that reason, the child will be left questioning the validity of every system. They may also be confused since the conflicting beliefs about the world pose different questions in their lives. Such children can also internalize a significant point of view that the world isn't safe. Therefore, they shall become isolated within themselves. If there is any form of response or emotional abuse coupled with trauma in the family, the child will undoubtedly lose their self-identity.

In past cases where an abusive group has denigrated independent thinking skills while creating dependency as well as insecurity within the personality of the child, no questions or protests were allowed by any means. In many abusive situations, the toddler was made to feel that they were unworthy in many ways. The child, being fearful, became abnormal and mistrustful of various authority figures, including teachers and the law enforcement body. Because they had been regarded as the enemy, these children would be unable to turn to their parents for help. As they went ahead to think as well as behave as often trained by their parents in the family structure, or better yet, the group, they stifled their initial personality while rejecting independent thoughts as selfish as well as disloyal. This had an impact on their lives as the child's self-perception was distorted. At the same time, a framework of guilt was created in their minds. These children ended up devaluing themselves and their feelings.

Children with strong temperaments were considered rebellious when not resistant. But such individuals may have ended up making a viably effective transition into the community following their relocation into a different environment. Part of understanding who they are can be as simple as finding out the basics of their tastes. For instance, what is an individual's personal color? What do they prefer to eat? Do they like dogs or cats? Do they prefer winter to summer? If such a person could go anywhere across this world, where would it be? These are some of the basic elements that can assist a child survivor in understanding that there's one original self with preferences such as likes, dislikes, and viewpoints.

The pseudo personality also entails a broad range of self-righteousness and a major cheating pattern in the relationship. Some may take advantage of others. To fully understand the pseudo personality, such individuals have five typical behaviors based on expert opinion and research. In this list, you'll realize that pseudo personalities have common traits. But the mentioned behaviors aren't to be used as a form of diagnosis as it may give an impeccable idea regarding why someone may have a pseudo personality.

According to Psychology Today, a pseudo personality refers to a person who has a grandiosity personality disorder coupled with a lack of empathy for others. Such an individual may also need admiration from others. These traits make a pseudo personality challenging to hang out with because they are always willing to control people. Besides, they are also ruthless in manipulating people to do as they wish. To assist in finding out if you or someone closer to you is a pseudo personality, a list of alarming patterns has been developed below:

- Self-importance
- A belief that they are more special than others
- The need for admiration on a different level
- Some sense of entitlement
- Lack of empathy
- Envy
- Arrogance

Also, people with pseudo personalities can easily be affected by criticism as well as defeat. Therefore, they may quickly react with disdain as well as anger. However, social withdrawal may also follow. They may have some sense of entitlement, leading them to disregard other people in many ways. As a result, relationships may be damaged. Although a pseudo personality can be an overachiever, the disorder can harm their performance due to their sensitivity to criticism.

The Challenges of Dealing with a Pseudo Personality

Understanding Their Fragile Ego Could Be a Major Challenge

A person with a pseudo personality has a self-inflated ego. Such an individual is usually self-absorbed to the extent of ignoring the needs of other people. Therefore, there may be no other additional gods in their world. Even in a case where such a person says they believe in a higher being, they may not fully acknowledge the presence of God. To them, ego rules everything. When dealing with a pseudo personality, it may be challenging to identify the ego of such a person as their ego loves pleasure as well as pain.

Comprehending Their Ability to Shift Gears from the Real to the False World

The idea that a glimpse of their face can determine someone's character hails from the ancient era of Greece. In the 18th century, it was known as a popularized idea used as a talking point in the intellectual circles of psychologists. In the world of pseudoscience, a person with a pseudo personality is known for shifting gears often. Such an individual can quickly change from grandiosity to behaving like a person who is often better than the rest. A person with a pseudo personality often hogs credit from the achievements of other people while milking the injured or misfortune.

At the same time, victimized pseudo personalities are constantly looking for a gullible individual that will easily believe their version of a story regardless of its realness or exaggeration. What such people claim is the fact that they have different calamities. These calamities may make them selfish and self-centered in several ways. It is essential to be aware of such personalities since they are manipulative. The moment they identify that you don't share in their emotions or pamper to them in a particularly preferred way, they shall eliminate you from their lives.

The Pseudo Personality Is Pretty Controlling

The pseudo personality is known to be controlling in many ways. As such, it doesn't destroy someone completely. It suppresses a person by dominating it. Also, it's known to want one thing at this moment and something else at a different moment. The pseudo personality is programmed to want to quest its thirst, which is usually the opposite of the normal personality. While the real personality wants to get out of the abuse, the pseudo is often programmed to stay. That's one major challenge of dealing with such a personality since it's always in control. With that said, as long as the programmed personality is in charge, you'll find it challenging to deal with a pseudo personality.

It May Be Challenging to Identify the Nitty-Gritty of a Pseudo Personality

Typically, the cult leader, also identified as the head of the pseudo personality, presents himself as an ideal role model in charge of the group. The individual can easily use manipulative tricks to make his life and other projects successful. The rest of the team members are led to believe that they would be happier if they lived like their leader. As a victim of such circumstances, you may find it challenging to identify such elements in a pseudo personality.

A Pseudo Personality Is a Professional Liar

A pseudo personality is a pathological liar. The individual tells lies as well as stories that may fall between delusions coupled with conscious lying. At times, they may believe their lies. Therefore, it becomes challenging to understand them, including how to deal with such issues where lies are involved. Some of these liars do it often that even experts specializing in psychology cannot tell what's happening.

Additionally, the professionals may not even understand the difference between the facts presented at the table and the fiction given. Being pathological liars, such individuals tend to approach you naturally in their quest to manipulate others. Not only are they creative but also original. They are also quick thinkers such that they do not exude common signs of telling lies, including pauses and avoidance. When questioned, a pseudo personality may reveal more than they have been asked without being specific regarding the question.

It May Be Difficult to Deal with Their Vicious Temper

A pseudo personality has a psychological construct that often describes a significant reaction to their injury. All too often, this is conceptualized as a considerable threat to their self-esteem and worth. With that said, a pseudo personality is known for having a vicious temper caused by a previous interaction with someone who may have wounded them. This is the case when the individual falls from grace in that even their hidden character is revealed. It's also the case when their value, as well as importance, is questioned. A pseudo personality injury is caused by distress. It may, therefore, lead to the dysregulation of behaviors. Since they have a vicious temper as well, they may keep such traits hidden from you.

The Pseudo Personality Will Always Play a Victim

Everyone has played a victim at some point in life. Some have blamed their siblings for something they may not have done. Others have even pointed the finger at a co-worker for messing up a task. While this may often be manipulative in many cases, it's also clear that people with a pseudo personality play the victim in different instances when they are guilty.

Breaking the Machination

A person with a pseudo personality is not someone you should be associating with. Because you'll sustain emotional as well as physical harm that you will never recover from. With that said, you may not realize that such individuals have the mentioned traits.

It is so prevalent in the US; there is a good chance that you may have encouraged many of such individuals to be in your life. Even if you didn't, you might not be in a position to spot them instantly. But, because of their potential to mask their characters, you'll find it necessary to identify specific aspects of their behavior.

Here are a few tips for breaking the machination:

- **Refuse to Engage with an Individual Who Has a Pseudo Personality**
  If you want to untangle yourself from the docket of a pseudo personality, then you can begin by refusing to associate with them. Dodge the emotional as well as physical harm that hails from dealing with them. To be more specific, the only way to deal with them is to evade them.

- **Establish If the Conversation Must Always Be Spearheaded by Them**
  If you want to identify a pseudo personality among your friends and family, consider assessing if they always direct all conversations towards themselves. This would imply that they are self-centered and focused on turning every angle of discussion towards what they would rather listen to. That way, you can easily detach yourself.

- **Understand That They Are Takers and Not Givers Most of the Time**
  In the world of psychology, there are givers, takers, as well as matchers. While the givers will always find out how they can be of help to others, takers will always focus on being the recipients. On the other hand, matchers will concentrate on playing tit for tat on many occasions. However, there's a twist to all aspects as there are instances when the givers behave like takers and vice versa. People with a pseudo personality behave like givers but take everything from their loved ones if only to find comfort.

This implies that if you're in a relationship with such an individual, you may end up forfeiting everything you have at the expense of the friendship, and they will be very unwilling to give back or reciprocate in any way. To be safe while relating to such individuals, you need to observe them from a distance.

Most of these dissociative phenomena aren't necessarily a result of symptomatic illnesses. However, they significantly represent a continuous outset of normal psycho-biological modulation coupled with incoming information which may be stored. As such, prolonged environmental stress associated with day-to-day life situations may interfere with the integrative functions of a child's personality. People exposed to such forces may end up adapting via dissociation.

Chapter 4 - Inner Child Healing

Every person is a result of their history. In other words, you are the person you are today because of the collective experiences in your past. Every encounter, every experience, thought, pain and decision have culminated in creating the person you are today. This is because of a dominant theory of development that asserts that we are products of our environments, including both social and physical environments and our internal environment in terms of thoughts and inner experiences. The significance of these facts is found in the role of the environment shaping who you are right from childhood. Psychologists believe that your formative years in childhood underpin who you become as an adult because your brain is most impressionable and fragile between the ages 0 to 7 years. Resulting in the formation of beliefs, ideas, and concepts of who you are and what you should do to gain acceptability within the family, friends, and the larger society.

While these processes are primarily subconscious, their significance in your life is much more gigantic than you would ever imagine. The absorbed childhood experiences stay with you through adulthood, existing not only in the subconscious but manifesting in day-to-day decisions and actions. It is within the context that the concept of the inner child emerges. While a person may want to disregard this concept as another fascination of pop psychology, it is relatively easy to notice its existence in your day-to-day life. The inner child is primarily a free spirit that loves fun, creativity, and imaginativeness. All these elements come to life at various times during day-to-day activities. However, a lack of awareness means that it is impossible to capture its presence. For instance, when you are mindful, you can notice the inner child when you lose yourself in fun activities, enjoy a game, or fondly reminisce on an old photo. The inner child is also evident when you focus on pleasing your parents and other family members.

How Does It Happen?

The inner child is thus regarded as the psyche that encapsulates your qualities as a child. Therefore, you can consider aspects such as curiosity, spontaneity, and joyfulness that characterized your childhood. Besides the rosy and happy memories, you can also subconsciously carry the burden of a wounded past based on the traumatic and scary encounters. The negative experiences have been found to scar and wound your inner child. Leaving long-lasting impacts on how you relate and engage with your environment.

A wounded inner child comes about as a result of the mental and psychological underdevelopment that is unequipped to deal with the emotions and feelings associated with most challenges that defined your childhood. In other words, in the absence of appropriate cognitive abilities to comprehend the dynamics of your environment, you end up with a buildup of unprocessed emotions that become a defining factor of your subconscious mind. According to psychologists, the embedded emotions become crucial markers in a person's life, often causing many difficulties in your relationships, behavior, and feelings.

The suppressed emotions often become evident in your life through your behavior, relations, and activities. This is because unresolved issues in your childhood are often apparent through projecting roles of significant figures in your childhood on current relationships. From a psychological point of view, this occurs because you subconsciously want to resolve your past issues by re-creating similar situations. To further appreciate this concept, you can consider the example of a person who has unresolved issues with their father. As such, they will project these feelings to their boss or any other authority figure. Suppressed emotions can also manifest in your life through numerous mental disorders, including identity problems, low self-esteem, psycho-sexual difficulties, and criminal behavior. Additionally, you may also notice instances of lack of belief and trust in yourself and others, the development of various addictions, and the lack of genuine friends in your life.

While these examples do not cover the entirety of aspects of a wounded inner child, they do offer crucial insights into how failing to address the inner child can directly affect the quality of your life. By appreciating the impact of unresolved and suppressed emotions in your life as well as the presence of your inner child, you are initiating a process of transformation like no other. Unlike the love and care you may show towards your child, pet, friend, or family member, acknowledging your inner child creates space for the onset of a transformational experience like no other. The liberation of your mind from the numerous mental and emotional burdens that define your current life lies in the ability to embrace your inner child. This is followed by a deliberate and conscious effort to initiate a healing process that will see you become whole again.

Therefore, the contact process is vital in the sense that it makes it possible for you to reinitiate the severed link to your inner child. As abstract as this may seem, your complete belief in this process offers unprecedented benefits for your current and future life. Contact is made through an objective reflective process designed to help you come to terms with the onset of your phase of pain life. Visualization is the most suitable in this regard. It involves picturing yourself as a child from as far back as you can remember and exploring the happy, sad, scary, or joyful moments that formed part of your childhood. Patience is in attaining this goal since it makes it possible for your brain to uncover the hidden emotions and experiences that characterize your upbringing. This process can take an hour or longer and should be done comprehensively to ensure that all perspectives have been brought to light.

By encountering the residual pain and negativity of your childhood experience, the feeling of hate is likely to arise. However, your focus should be on uncovering the underlying emotions rather than reacting to them. This will mean maintaining a sense of compassion and understanding for yourself and those that might have inflicted the pain. By understanding and validating the pain to wash over your body, you are primarily taking charge of an experience you locked out for years. It is at this point that you must talk to your inner child. While this is pure imagination and visualization, it does help your subconscious mind to reveal some of the underlying challenges and how they continue to hamper your life. Creating space for communication and conversation with your inner child makes it possible for the adult brain to process past experiences and pain for better outcomes.

The process of introspection as an adult makes it possible for proper organization and cohesiveness in your narrative of life. With the capacities attained by your adult mind, the brain can reframe your childhood experiences with the realization that your tormentors might have been victims of abuse as well. The change of perspective goes a long way in helping you reconnect your body, mind, and soul. The sensations and feelings that have been suppressed for years may create a gap in emotional experiences. As an adult, this gap can cause a crisis of identity manifested in various maladaptive behaviors and tendencies. The reconnection process is used to integrate the new processed story into your subconscious mind.

The reconnection process is the culmination of your healing journey in that it allows your cells, consciousness, and soul to embody a new and coherent narrative that has been formed out of the logical process, compassion, and forgiveness. This process should then be cemented through the process of consolation. The consolation process involves the commitment to upholding the reestablished relationship. As you become aware of the outer environment, your imagination must focus on reminding the inner child of the continued relationship that will ensue from the reconciliation process. This means the care and attention necessary to nurture the inner child will continue.

The Inner Child in Adulthood

It is vital that you are awakening to the fact that the existence of the inner child is an inherent part of your life. The fact that you once were a child means that you still embody the memories and experiences of this period of your life, though unconsciously. The unappreciated fact of life is that many so-called adults have their age as the core factor of their adulthood. Still, psychologically, they remain insecure and oblivious of who they are. True maturity is defined by the ability to take responsibility for nurturing your inner child with the care and attention that characterizes any effective parenting process. In the absence of proper care and attention, as is the case with neglect and suppression that characterizes most adult reactions to the inner child, subtle symptoms emerge.

Your inner child encapsulates the innocence, wonder, joy, and sensitivity that defines childhood experiences. The inner child is also made up of the fears and traumas that might have defined your upbringing. By rejecting or denying your inner child, not only do you eliminate the positive qualities and potential the inner child represents but that you also wrongly assume that you have outgrown your negative childhood experiences. As a result, while you might regard yourself as mature, at the core of your being, you still harbor your little self, though unconsciously. In essence, most of your decisions emanate from a fearful and highly traumatized child despite the so-called adulthood you have gained over time.

As has been pointed out time and again, the challenge for many adults is in the absence of awareness of the inner child. This unconsciousness facilitates the subtle intrusion of the disenchanted inner child in day-to-day decisions and behaviors. Therefore, for adults, the first step of peacefully coexisting with your inner child involves becoming conscious that your younger self is still very much a part of you, as are your soul and mind. With this acknowledgment, a psychological adult must take the time to appreciate the message and significance of their inner child. In other words, while you might agree with this concept intellectually, its impact on your life will only manifest once you begin to take your inner child seriously.

Guided by the primal needs that define childhood, such as love, protection, and understanding, you must begin to communicate and engage with your inner child. Therefore, the mark of adulthood is in accordance with the willingness to become aware of the insufficiencies of childhood and the time and effort necessary to transmute these shortcomings. The gist of adulthood is that it comes with experience and the capacity for logical thinking. As a result, this means that your adult personality can easily learn and adopt new skills. In this regard, you are at liberty to establish a new relationship with your inner child based on compassion and understanding. As is the case with parenting a flesh-and-blood child, you must assume a similar stance in approaching your inner child. This means developing boundaries, organized structures as well as the necessary disciplines to guide behavioral tendencies. Such an approach ultimately results in a cooperative and mutually beneficial relationship between your inner child and your adult self.

What Does a Stable Childhood Look Like?

It is pointless to discuss the process of healing your inner child without looking at some of the defining factors that make up a stable childhood. In other words, without understanding what you may have missed in your upbringing, it may be impossible to pinpoint the exact wounds you may have accumulated during your childhood. The overarching concept about a stable childhood involves the freedom of exploration, the safety, and security of guardianship, as well as the attention and care for your fragile soul and mind. In other words, your childhood should comprise an understanding of family, supportive friends and relatives, and most importantly, a safe and ordered society. These three tenets underpin the fundamental dynamics of a stable childhood experience.

At the family level, you learn about freedom, independence, love, and attention. The home environment should be a safe space where you are fully protected, cared for, and appreciated. With imagination and creativity bubbling through your mind as a child, you also require time to play and explore various limits of your abilities. This proves vital in helping you identify your interests and strengths as well as weaknesses. A child must also learn the importance of teamwork, sharing, and respect. These values are primarily adopted during group play with other children. The freedom to venture beyond the house walls is thus a vital tenet of a stable upbringing. As the child is exposed to different perspectives, they gain new perspectives and begin to understand who they are and what they stand for.

Rules, structure, and organization are also essential for your childhood. With limited cognitive capacities as a child, you often lack the ability to analyze and appreciate the gravity of various experiences and encounters. It is for this reason that the family social environment must offer some sort of order and structure. The discipline and structures adopted within the family and large social circle prove vital in helping children appreciate the importance of standing up for something worthwhile. Besides enjoying loads of fun, children also need to feel loved and cared for. Parents and guardians must be willing to create time for their children when the child is the main focus of attention. Dotting on your child allows them to integrate the fact that they are loved and that they can always have somewhere to run to in cases of trouble. While seemingly insignificant, these tenets define who you are as an adult since they are embedded deep inside your subconscious mind.

Caring for Your Inner Child

The purpose of understanding your inner child in adulthood, as well as the definition of a stable childhood, is to help you come to terms with the fact that you could be harboring a wounded inner child while remaining unaware. Once you have established this, the healing process can be initiated, as has been stipulated before. You have to understand that just as it is challenging to nurture and raise a child, so will the process of healing your inner child. Patience, commitment, and determination are three vital ingredients that will help you emerge from the pool that you have been downing in all your life. It is important to note that you must assume the duty and responsibility of caring for your inner child upon healing old wounds.

Neglect and denial offer no meaningful solutions, and as such, in the absence of sustained care, you may develop abandonment of your inner child and continue the suppression of emotions.

Identifying Childhood Pain

The identification of the root cause of your pain is the very beginning of a life-transforming journey. The willingness and commitment to transmute your pain into meaningful and progressive energy must start at the point of origin. As pointed out earlier, visualization is a vital tenet in this particular effort; more importantly, however, is the need for meditation. By consciously exploring the depths of your subconscious mind with a focus on childhood experience, you encounter some of your past's joyous and painful experiences. Within this particular context, you will come face to face with pain and hurt that defined your upbringing.

Re-Parenting Your Inner Child

As is the case with your child, sibling, or relative, guidance, care, and attention underpin the process of healing the inner child. In other words, you must be ready to undertake the slow and gradual process of letting yourself come to terms with your past. This will allow you to reestablish safe and healthy ties with your inner child. As an adult, you must undertake this process, realizing that your mental, physical, and psychological health hinge upon the success of this particular endeavor. While professional help is often encouraged when it comes to establishing new ties with your inner child, the process can be achieved single-handedly by adopting approaches that define the nurturing of an actual child.

Therefore, the re-parenting process is dotted with affirmations that remind you of your true values and ideals, as well as self-talks that serve to address various issues and challenges that arise in day-to-day experiences. As is the case with taking care of a child, you must also offer yourself rewards for achievements and improvements arising from the commitment of newer and stronger relations. Finally, a sense of mindfulness underpins the re-parenting process. Staying aware of the experiences and encounters of the present is vital in reconciling your past and present. This eliminates the psychological dissonance that might arise subconsciously and thus influence your decisions and behavior.

Engaging Your Inner Child

Listening and talking to your inner child are effective ways of engaging with who you were as a child and how you can relate as a better human being. Engagement efforts encompass activities such as listening and talking to your inner child or more detailed methods such as writing to yourself. Talking and listening to yourself helps you come to terms with the needs of your inner child. With this information, you will be able to initiate meaningful changes in your behavior to make it possible for the inner child to thrive. Engagement with your inner child must focus on the original fears and issues that might have been present in your childhood. More importantly, however, to guide the inner child to the present. In other words, the talk should focus on helping the inner child appreciate the transformations that have arisen and how the past shaped who you are as a person in the present.

Chapter 5 - Creating Your Thoughts

Thinking availability is very vital when it comes to developing your reality. Anything that you will think of in the physical world will have some clues from your thinking and perceptions inside. You can be the boss of your intention when you control the thoughts you have and their dominance. When you do that, you will experience knowing the truth behind your thinking and how you come up with authenticity. Many people believe that they can't have control over what they are thinking. You can find yourself having flowing thoughts in your mind that are brought about by an invisible force. You are advised not to have mercy with your inner thoughts as they will stem your ego and bring about minor issues. When you get to know how to control your dreams, this will bring about enacting what you want and feel is the best.

Awareness

The first thing you to do for having control over your views is by identifying undesirable patterns. Unless you are sure of determining the negative impacts in your thoughts, you won't be able to develop the positive effects. You can as if you are assessing some activities. Get back deep in your mind and listen to your inner mockery and try to determine whether it's a hurdle to your capability to have fun in life. Hearing your thoughts can be the first practice because you are well conversant with your inner voice that comes along with your character due to the background distractions.

Occasionally, you will be able to identify some detailed thoughts more so when you hold on to your activities for a period and pause. Nevertheless, most of your life is spent in action and not being, thus making you on autopilot and engrossed in involvement with full consciousness. Being on autopilot, you can still influence your feelings by your opinions despite not being attentive to their presence. With this, your inner voice will insistently notify you that life is negative; thus, you will have negativity in your focus. Your knowledge will bring out uncertainties that shoot from cynical intellectuals.

Hearing of the Inner Voice

You need to learn how to listen to your inner voice when you are alone and try to know what is going through your brain. You will get to know this as you wait for your thoughts, and this may often occur when your inner voice goes silent. There will be some discovery on the spaces amid your thoughts where peace and healing can come from. When there is an appearance of ideas, you are advised not to judge them, thus offering them some moments to develop then pay attention. Try to find out whether your inner voice is critical or expressing distress. You can still get to know whether your thoughts are positive and have appreciation and gratitude.

Negative and positive thinking

When you think of appreciating, you will be able to make up happiness and bring forth greater joy to your life. When this is formed in your brain, you have to amplify this and bring it to your heart, where it will have a sharp point. When you have negative thoughts, you will likely be advised to soothe your inner being by compassion. Don't let yourself be mad anytime you feel your inner part is not the way you want it to be. Perhaps you should send a feeling of love from your heart and make the negativity inside you billow away as you keep your focus on positive subjects.

5 Steps to Regain Control of Your Thoughts

Thoughts are considered to be either our best friend or our worst enemy, and this is according to a Buddhist monk Matthieu Ricard. At least every individual has had a moment when their minds have minds of their own, but still controlling their thoughts, thus enhancing happiness, reduced stress, and being well equipped in problem-solving and achieving goals. A lot of individuals are not always informed of what they are thinking about.

Similarly, you will be your observer and controller of your thoughts' impacts on yourself. You may find yourself being depressed, mad, frustrated, sad, among others. Some simple steps below will help you in controlling your thoughts and stopping negative thinking.

1. **Study How to Prevent Your Thoughts**
   You have to learn how to put it on hold when you are in the middle of your thoughts. It may be a dull, harmful, or useful idea. Most of the time during the day, you will find yourself thinking. When you feel frustrated, mad, or tired about certain things, you will have some tendency of still pressing on in whatever feeling you have; thus, this isn't an advisable approach. You will become more irresponsible, more emotional, and you will tend to be angrier. You can quickly see such in others and not often in yourself. When you have children, try to think of how your children behave when they get mad and irritated. If you do not have children, then think of the behavior of a friend's child, or you can also have the option of thinking about a person you know who is temperamental.

   Think deeply for five minutes about your thoughts before pressing on.

2. **Recognize Negative Feelings Within You**
   When you can stop your beliefs, then this will assist you with times ahead. You can first evaluate yourself on how you are feeling. Every feeling you are having is directly from the outcome of something you were thinking.
   For instance, if you are feeling anxious, you can question yourself as to why, and taking some steps back will identify what has caused the feeling of anxiousness. You may be having

a project deadline to meet or going to fire somebody; thus. By thinking about what is making you worried and trying to find the main problem of your anxiety. In any case, know that whatever is making you anxious will be the reason your brain is creating an emotional mood. Though at times, it's not the primary cause of your emotional state.

3. **Note down Your Mental Tape**
   With the previous step correctly done, you can recognize the movie that is in your mind. This can be a meeting that your boss chewed on you. It can also be the time when you flopped during a presentation. You can also be disturbed by the voice of your dad, telling you how worthless you are. A lot of people have negative mental tapes that bring about negativity canceling positive tapes. There is a time where current situations will make you replay the previous status of that movie. You can have five successful occurrences and one disappointment, and your mind will want to get to the frustration because of the need to avoid pain than seek pleasure. All you are required to do is identify the content of the tape then note it down. This will help you get it out of your mind.

   Writing it down will get it outside your brain, and you will have distanced yourself from the sentiments that it makes. This can be referred to as dissociation, and when you note down your mental tapes, this is part of it. You will find it a straightforward process because you need a pen and paper. When you dissociate yourself from something, then it's like you have excluded yourself from the first-person spot in the brain. If you are to be asked about a painful experience in the past to think about like it's happening, then you will be able to take yourself back to that condition. This can bring up feelings, thus making you angry, sad, among many other emotions. This is known as associates. You are placing yourself in an event. On most occasions, the mental tapes play will take us back to the situation of pain. When you note down your mental tapes it will remove you from associating with anxiety, giving you some steps to move out of the situation. This step will be a positive step in helping you calm down. When you remove the tapes from your mind, it will also remove their power.

4. **Get the Lie**

    In every mental tape, there is a lie about yourself on what you choose to believe, whether deliberately or subconsciously. You should be able to find what the myth is, and this is a significant step. The lie can be that you are a nobody or a failure in life, amongst many other things. You can sometimes experience it as someone told you; for example, no woman would love you. You have to inscribe it in your mental tape fast.

5. **Find the Truth**

    You will want to combat the myth; thus, the only solution is to find out the truth about yourself. You can be in prayers, reading your Bible, and trying to inquire from God what He destined you to be. There are different processes you can use. You can decide to talk to friends about it or seek advice from your coach. It doesn't matter the route you will take as long as you get to the truth. When you find the truth, then you can write it next to the lie. Put it in the first person and phrase it positively. Instead of that, noting it down like "you are not a failure," you can phrase it, "you are a better individual full of positive impacts." Even the Bible talks about this in Philippians 4:8.

Get Rid of The Poor Self-Concept of Your Thoughts

Seeing yourself unworthy, incompetent, a failure, known as having low self-esteem. Such opinions will create negative thoughts that can easily affect your life decisions, thus decreasing your esteem. You can decide to use some of the tools of mindfulness as you study other situations without it negatively influencing your past.

Live in the Moment

With a good focus on time, you will likely have to select your moves wisely and precisely. This will be done without affecting your past, not reflecting on any worries but having positive hopes about the future.

Create Awareness

When you are aware, you will quickly recognize how you are reacting and tackling your uncertainties, making a moment amid your feelings and activities. You are then expected to answer more healthily.

Inscribe in a Journal

A lot of your views and feelings have been locked in your hidden mind, and inscribing can assist you in bringing them into your alertness. Writing what you feel and think can help you sort negative concepts about yourself from the truth of who you are in reality.

Don't Judge

Approaching your life without judging will make you accept yourself, your involvements, disappointments, and achievements, as well as what people say about you without being worried if it's good or bad and if you agree or disgrace.

Be Connected to Yourself

When you are mindful, it can assist you to enhance a sense of connecting with yourself, reducing the need to being a people pleaser; trying to please everybody without setting boundaries means that you will satisfy other individuals and forget about your wants.

Enhance Watchful Meditation

When you are meditating, it merely means you are letting go of the competing thoughts in your concentration and tolerating that those feelings and beliefs are temporary rather than parts of yourself. You must try to preserve some moments daily to be still and focus on your conscious mind and watch your worries billow away like clouds.

Have Participation in Your Personal Life

Mindfulness inspires us to become lively and confident in enhancing our own experiences. Knowing your thoughts and selecting your replies will permit you to act and take part in your personal life.

Advanced Beginner's Mind

With a beginner's mind, you will look at things like you are sighting them for the first time with a lot of sincerity, enthusiasm, and liberty from anticipation. You will see things in a new light rather than robotically retorting with the old patterns of character.

Let Go

The goal of being mindful is either non-attachment or letting go. Letting go of what you are thinking of or what you should do, you can trust yourself and decide on what you feel is right for you.

Have Compassion to Yourself

You are supposed to have love towards yourself as much as anyone else. When you have self-compassion, you will be able to give yourself love, protection, and the reception you want.

Refocus Your Mind

Having a wandering brain will be beneficial and is achievable. When you are enhancing your mental focus, it may not be fast and straightforward. If it would have been easy, then all of us would be very sharp and attentive. Some ideas can help you enhance your mental focus and attentiveness.

Begin by Assessing your Mental Focus

You have to know the strength of your mental focus before you begin working on enhancing your mental focus. Your focus will be great if you find it simple to be alert, set goals and try breaking your tasks into smaller parts, take short rests, and then get back to work. Your focus should be worked on if you are regularly daydreaming, can't identify obstacles, and quickly lose your level of progress. You will probably have an excellent attention ability with more learning if your statements are like your style. If your focus has to be worked on, you will have to be strict on your mental focus enhancement. This can take time, but you can be assisted by learning good habits and being stable in your mind.

Eradicate Interferences

You have to accept that you saw this phrase coming. It can be healthy, but many people have underestimated how so many interferences have hindered them from being attentive to the tasks they have at hand. Such distractions can come from loud background music.

Controlling such disturbances can make things more relaxed, but still, there are some challenges you are supposed to handle. A simple way of dealing with this is by just excusing yourself and requesting to be left alone for some time and getting some specific time just for yourself. You can also go somewhere that you won't have any distractions and work peacefully. Places like libraries, your house, or a silent coffee shop can be good places to give a try. You may try to rest before handling any task to help you fight off anxiety and worry; thus, you will need positive thoughts. When your mind has focused on distractions, you have to bring it back to the work you have at hand.

Put Your Focus on One Thing at a Time

When having several tasks at hand, you will tend to work fast to finish; thus, this may lead to poorly completing the functions. Doing so many jobs at once will decrease your productivity, thus making you leave some essential ideas out. Think of your focus like a spotlight that shines at a particular area; you have clear visibility, unlike when you cross it in a dark room where you won't have a clear vision. To improve your focus, enhance the resources you have and stop doing so many things at once, and therefore focus on one task at a time.

Be in the Moment

You may find it tiresome to be focused mentally when due to other reasons, you are still thinking of the past. At some point, you have been able to encounter people talking about being present. This is when you are supposed to put away all the distractions and fully concentrate mentally on the current moment. The notion of staying present is vital for recollecting your mental focus. When you are fully engaged, you will be attentive and get the essential points at that particular time. It may take some duration to study how to be at the moment. You cannot change what occurred in the past, and the future has not happened yet; thus, what you do at this moment in time will assist you in avoiding your past errors, making way for a great future.

Exercise Mindfulness

This is an important topic to cover, and many people have studied how to be mindful for many years and its health benefits, but it has recently started to be fully understood. There is a study where professionals engaged humans to assist in completing many complex tasks in a day. The jobs had to be completed within 20 minutes; an example of the tasks included picking up calls, planning meetings. When you are training about mindfulness, then you will involve yourself in how to undertake methodically. You might consider the job to be simple, but it is often more complicated than it appears. With time, you will know that it's easier to bring your focus to where it is supposed to be.

Take a Small Break

You have probably been in a situation where you have been undertaking a task for a long time, and then your focus breaks down with time; thus, you will be in a problematic condition trying to bring back your mental focus to the task at hand. This will significantly affect your performance too. It is advisable that anytime you have an elongated responsibility, try and give yourself a short break. Try shifting your attention to something different just for a duration. The break will provide you with a sharp mental focus, enabling you to have a high-performance impact on your task.

Practice More to Strengthen Your Focus

Building your mental focus will not be built quickly, as there are so many steps to go through. Sports professionals also need time to practice and help in firming their intent skills. You will note your impact when you first try to recognize that distraction will affect your life. When you find yourself consumed by other unimportant issues, you have to focus more on giving yourself time. When you enhance your focus, you will achieve so many things in life like success, happiness, and fulfillment.

Tips for Improving Mindfulness

Techniques that can help in enhancing awareness of the current moment are:

1. **Just Respire**

   When you are seated, try being mindful of your breath. Try and concentrate on how the belly is rising; this will make you focus and be aware. Try and focus on your breathing when you are waiting for a bus, when in a traffic jam, when waiting to eat, among others. When you have a single breath purposefully, this can be a great way to enhance mindfulness.

2. **Take a Walk**

   By getting up and having a walk with purpose and awareness. Go somewhere attractive where you can go and walk and get to spend any minute to acknowledge. Try looking at the muscles in your legs and toes as they move and carry your body. You can try to make walking meditation your day-to-day routine.

3. **Enjoy Being in Silence**

   The best condition for achieving mindfulness is quietness. Teach yourself to enact and explore it. Your life is always calm, but you still get some distractions that fill that void, like music, a ring of a phone, traffic sounds, and airplanes above. You have to be silent and try to explore during that time. Try to get to understand feelings of anxiety that often arise and making you forgo your distractions.

How to Affirm Yourself

1. **Remove Selfish and Cynical Individuals in Your Life**

    Stay away from individuals with negativity and those who will bring stress and sadness to your life. You are advised not to cut them from your life completely. This is understandable because it can be impossible. You have to avoid making them your priority and get to them when you are right. You will find it very difficult to have confidence in the people who treated you badly and never appreciated you. When you are choosing your friends, upgrade your standards.

2. **Have Goals and Achieve Them**

    You have to get some breakthroughs before you reach specific points on enhancing the quality of your life. It doesn't matter if goals are big or small as long as you achieve them. These are the level, and you will realize your efforts are paying off and bringing you nearer to your desires. Always try improving different categories in your life, thus bringing more improvement.

3. **Expand Yourself**

    One of the most significant hurdles that one faces in having confidence is being unemployed. When you are not employed, you will have financial strains and a lot of issues to handle. Instead of having some sympathy for yourself about being jobless, try taking time to enhance yourself and with information and aids. Evaluate yourself, try to do things you are interested in, and spend a good time with the people you love. Make sure you can create connections that can be positively great in giving you opportunities.

4. **Have Time to Assist Others**

When you do positive things for others, then it will bring a positive impact on yourself. You will have to realize that making someone happy will help enhance the life of someone and inspire others. When you affirm yourself, it's just not about you but trying to be kind and helpful to others. These ideas will help enhance yourself.

Chapter 6 - Survival Mode

So, you have found yourself as a victim of a severe narcissist; whether domestic, parental, or work-related, walking away is a viable option. Other people may not understand why you did it, but how could they without deep insight into your partner?

It may trouble you trying to understand why your partner did the things they did and how they did them. Didn't they care about the relationship? Didn't they care about you? These are common thoughts that may continuously cross your mind. When you find that you are consumed with these negative, sad thoughts, remind yourself that it is possible to forget and live being a stronger and smarter person.

Is it PTSD?

Victims of narcissistic abuse exhibit psychological symptoms of post-traumatic stress disorder (PTSD). Unlike PTSD caused by a single traumatic event, narcissistic trauma is a separate clinical term for severe, repetitive, prolonged trauma- complex PTSD, or C-PTSD. The survivors appear to be disconnected and unaware of their emotional anguish and pain-ridden thoughts. When the victim of abuse can receive validation of the reality of their experience, the cognitive dissonance abates and dissolves.

Complex PTSD usually involves emotional or physical torture, for example, childhood trauma, domestic violence, or even sexual abuse. Because the abuser forms a biochemical bond with their victim, it becomes exceedingly challenging to detach yourself from them. However, that does not mean that suffering is not real or severe. Unfortunately, there have been instances where a victim of covert emotional abuse is driven to commit suicide. Society is uncertain of how to deal with the narcissist partners and survivors.

The abuser struggles to demonstrate the absurdity of the victim's reality claims. This sort of psychological warfare takes on a lasting effect on the survivor's brain due to chronic psychological trauma. There is often much breaking up and making up in the relationship because the narcissist does not seek help, nor does the survivor. The survivor may fail to report the abuse because of fear of the unknown and the risk of not being believed and understood by society. Also, survivors struggle with protecting their self-worth and protecting their abusers.

How Can You Tell if You Have C-PTSD?

Often victims of narcissistic abuse experience self-worthlessness and seek to correct their characteristic flaws pointed out by the abuser. Persons suffering from this type of abuse are often obsessed with their shortcomings and failures in the relationship, not as they have experienced but as the abuser has outlined them. Their thoughts are regularly beating them up and self-condemning. They may say, "It's my fault, really," "I cannot blame him for yelling at me," "I am the reason she is having an affair." It is common for them to beat themselves up for the actions of their abusers.

Narcissistic abuse survivors suffer symptoms including:

Intrusive depressing thoughts

The intrusive thoughts may manifest in memories of traumatic events, nightmares, and upsetting dreams containing aspects of the traumatic episodes. They may also occur as flashbacks, leading to loss of consciousness and increased physiological effects such as a rapid heart rate after exposure to triggers.

Stress

Exposure to trauma can lead the victim to cause serious injury to themselves or others, commit suicide, or project sexual violence to others. Direct witnesses to these circumstances may also succumb to stress factors.

Avoidance

People who have been through a troubling series of events are prone to avoid reminders of the trauma. They tend to keep away from external reminders such as people, places, activities, and even conversations. They also block thoughts that may remind them of the trauma they suffered.

Exclusion

Survivors tend to detach and isolate themselves from close friends and relatives as well as social activities. Dissociation is expected from a victim of trauma as it is the mind's way of recovering.

Changes in Arousal and Reactivity

The trauma triggers may worsen after the victim has detached from the abuser and abusive situations. For example, the survivor may become more irritable or aggressive, easily alarmed, and hyperattentive. They may also exhibit trouble concentrating and sleeping, as well as show some self-destructive behavior.

Difficulty Controlling Emotions

The victim may experience difficulty controlling negative thoughts and feelings, such as depression, anger, and irritability.

Altered Perception of Self and World

The abuser shapes the victim's entire existence. They rewrite their previous beliefs about themselves and the world to the views of their abuser. Their self-worthlessness is drilled into them, and so their self-image becomes distorted. They experience feelings of helplessness, guilt, and shame. They view the world and themselves negatively.

Obsession with the Abuser

The survivors may develop an unhealthy obsession with their abusers. They become codependent- like one another's drug. They put their emotional, psychological and physical health aside to appease the abuser. The obsession may go as far as the victim plotting revenge against the abuser. They become consumed with their abuser and let the feelings they elicit foster.

Difficulty with Personal Relationships

They may experience trouble forging friendships or relationships outside the abuser. For example, current relationships may disintegrate because of exclusion. They may find it difficult to interact with other people due to their new perception of themselves and their world.

Studies have shown that this kind of trauma survivors suffer mental death because they have been victimized so long that they lose their pre-trauma identity.

Anyone can develop post-traumatic stress disorder- at any age. The risk factors that increase the risk of PTSD include:
- Holidays and anniversaries

- Getting hurt or seeing another person hurt
- Feeling helplessness or horror
- Stress
- Little or no social support
- Childhood trauma, and
- History of mental illness or substance abuse

In addition to these symptoms, it may be common to feel like the victim is not ready to forgive. The victim must not rush into recovery, as there is a need to relearn most of the emotions and emotional cues, such as:
- Hope
- Trust
- Limits and boundaries
- Regaining back life
- Gratitude and happiness
- Rebuilding friendships and
- Self-love

Getting Help

If you have PTSD from a complicated relationship, seeking validation of your experiences to heal is necessary. Keeping a journal is an excellent way to track your emotions and other physical and psychological changes to your body.

Deteriorating C-PTSD symptoms can lead to a decline in your quality of life. If you experience these symptoms for longer than four weeks, you must seek professional help. If gone untreated, patients find unhealthy, destructive coping habits like substance abuse. It is not necessarily true that time heals all wounds. Seeking professional help ensures that a proper physical and psychological evaluation is conducted to eliminate any symptoms caused by pre-existing conditions. A good evaluation also aims to define your symptoms for correct diagnosis.

Recovery from abuse needs the integration of the cognitive, psychological, and emotional parts of the brain. Three necessary conditions are; maintaining a safe space meaning a trauma-free zone, recollecting the circumstances and mourning the past, and reconnection with your new life.

Some resilience factors that may minimize the risk of suffering PTSD include:

Finding a Support Group

Finding support works as a safety plan to help you deal with stressful situations. It is an excellent strategy to plan in case you are confronted with a psychologically draining circumstance. Make a list of emergency contacts whom you can dial should you feel the need.

Identify Early Warning Triggers

Warning signs often precede symptoms. Anticipating warning signs and triggers such as negative thoughts, changes in mood, and behavior can help you learn how to manage them better to avoid PTSD relapse as you heal. For example, you may be triggered by hearing a frustrated someone shouting at a person, a pet, or even a machine. Other external triggers, such as hearing a song that marks a traumatic stage in your life. Mental preparation to deal with unforeseen triggers eliminates panic and helps you cope easier.

Identify Coping Methods

Once you have identified the internal and external warning signs, it is time to whip out your most preferred coping method for that particular trigger. For example, you can write several step-by-step coping cards that you can carry with you in case of a trigger. Let's say you hear that song that reminds you of dark times, calmly retrieve your cards, and see which coping strategy works best to relax you. There are also a variety of software applications that can help cater for stress and anxiety management.

Recovery is best done with the right combination of clinical, family, and peer support. Helping a C-PTSD survivor goes beyond PTSD treatment into assisting them to regain power, self-control, and self-identity. C-PTSD is not yet well recognized by medical practitioners, as it needs to be diagnosed and treated differently from other mental disorders and PTSD. Its treatment focuses mainly on therapy, standard behavioral therapies, and exposure therapies. Medication is also prescribed for extreme cases.

Psychotherapy

In the confines of a safe space, a clinician or therapist will encourage you to talk about the trauma you experienced. This form of therapy is conducted either on a one-on-one basis or as group treatment. To achieve a well-rounded treatment, the therapist may combine different approaches depending on your individual needs, focusing on the symptoms or concentrating on your social life, family, work, and relationships.

Psychotherapy takes about 7 to 14 weeks, where the patient gradually learns to trust the therapist. The therapist, in turn, helps the patient identify their symptoms and triggers and develop healthy coping mechanisms. Psychotherapy helps the patient learn
- about trauma and its effects
- how to relax in high-stress situations
- tips and tricks to a healthy lifestyle and sleep patterns
- how to deal with emotions of shame, guilt, and helplessness, among others.

Cognitive-Behavioral Therapy

This is one example of therapy treatments that help the patients to remain mindful of their moods and bodily sensations and how to deal with them as they arise. This type of therapy also educates the patient's family members on recognizing and dealing with a C-PTSD survivor.

Exposure therapy is a form of CBT that involves gradually exposing yourself to already experienced trauma but in a safe "controlled" environment. The patient may revisit these traumas by visualizing, writing, or visiting places where the trauma occurred. This strategy helps the survivors face their fears and overcome them.

Cognitive restructuring therapy pairs well with exposure therapy. Often victims of trauma link people, places, things, and events with negative thoughts. Cognitive restructuring helps them healthily rewrite these thoughts by replacing the negative thoughts about these places with a more objective one. With the therapist's help, patients can take another rational look at situations and free themselves of pent-up emotions about it.

Eye movement desensitization and reprocessing (EMDR) therapy involves some factors of psychotherapy that are used to relieve traumatic triggers in small doses as the therapist directs your eye movement with rhythmic right-left stimulation. By diverting your attention while recollecting traumatic events, you are prone to have reduced psychological reactions to these memories. With time, the disturbing memories will have little to no impact on you. Multiple studies have shown that EMDR helps treat PTSD and other mental conditions such as depression, stress, anxiety, eating disorders, and addictions.

Medications

Although no C-PTSD medications are approved, some medicines are prescribed together with psychotherapy to alleviate the symptoms, but they do not treat the disorder. Antidepressants are a conventional treatment for PTSD symptoms. The patients should remain honest in the subjective diagnosis for the doctor to arrive at the best combination of medication for them. A variety of antipsychotics, antidepressants, and anti-anxiety medication helps the patient manage C-PTSD symptoms or recurrent disorders that may arise because of or alongside it.

Along with treatment, it is also beneficial to help yourself. It isn't easy to take that first step into recovery, but it is the most vital step. Take care of yourself and expect your symptoms to improve over time. Engaging in physical activity is an excellent way to get moving. Exercises release feel-good hormones that help you relax. You could also immerse yourself in comforting social situations, you may feel uneasy at first, but it gradually gets better and more comfortable. Try to confide in a close family member or friend.

Gratitude Exercises

"Gratitude drives happiness. Happiness boosts productivity. Productivity unveils mastery. And, mastery motivates the world."- Robin Sharma.

Exercising gratitude is a powerful human emotion. Gratitude occurs in many forms; you could be thanking The Almighty, Mother Nature, yourself, whomever. Thankfulness comes easy to survivors of trauma, and exercising it for even a short period can cause a notable improvement in your health and life.

Trauma causes psychopathological conditions and strips away your happiness. The relationship between gratitude and joy is multifaceted. Although happiness is a genetic factor, people tend to fall back to a particular level of happiness through gratitude exercises, it can be improved. For example, you could send a thank you note to your close friend or family member for their constant support. You will find that this act of kindness will considerably improve your mood.

Gratitude exercises not only increase your level of happiness but also improves your health. Studies have shown a notable connection between gratitude and good psychological and physical health. "Positive psychology" research shows that cultivating positive thoughts, habits, and beliefs may impact post-trauma symptoms like stress equally.

In addition to happiness, gratitude restores your former level of functioning. For example, if your work has been suffering due to C-PTSD, you could return to your productive kick-ass self by perhaps keeping a gratitude journal. Grateful employees are more effective, efficient, and more responsible. Employees who express gratitude create a sense of camaraderie in the company's productivity.

While anxiety is a valuable mechanism that the body uses to alert you of lurking danger and deployment of the fight or flight responses, it becomes harmful when it is unbridled. By a conscious effort to exercise gratitude, you retrain the brain to select only the positive images, and outcomes hence reduce anxiety. A study conducted with a large group of men showed that a grateful outlook on life allows us to gain acceptance without fear of the future. Gratitude exercises are especially useful in treating phobias.

As a trauma survivor, make a conscious effort to set aside some time every day to express gratitude. Perhaps you are grateful from time to time, but setting daily reminders goes a long way into cultivating positive thoughts and habits. Being thankful every day helps you cope better with traumatic memories.

Here are small exercises to help you cultivate joy and happiness:

Compliments to myself	People I am grateful for
Current assets	Current challenges

Appreciate Yourself

Self-appreciation improves mood. Look at yourself in the mirror and shower yourself with compliments on your current efforts, past achievements, skills or abilities, and virtues. You may also include your physique- be thankful for your chiseled nose, long neck, etc. Use positive words like brave, strong, beautiful, and the like. Notice that your mood gets better with every adjective.

Keep a Gratitude Journal

Psychotherapists highly recommend expressive writing. Make your gratitude journal personal. You may prefer to write long journal entries or just a shortlist. A daily record is proof that dedicated, intentional gratitude improves the quality of life. Your journal entry may take the following format.

Journal sample A tip to journaling successfully is to focus on pouring your thoughts on paper as opposed to writing "well." Take some time to think about the things to which you are grateful. Be as descriptive as possible.

Schedule a Gratitude Visit

If you have someone to whom you feel you feel grateful, visit them. This exercise will help you purposefully express your gratitude. Let the person know that they are important to you in this journey.

Make a Gratitude Jar

In this exercise, you must place the jar strategically so that you are reminded to be grateful once the day, if not twice a day. You may choose to place it beside the bed or near your toothbrush in the bathroom. You can also choose to decorate the jar with attractive features that remind you to be grateful.

Laugh Out Loud

Suppose you find yourself stressed or having negative thoughts, burst into laughter for a complete minute. Laughing releases feel-good hormones that relax you. This is an excellent way to distract yourself from sudden unwelcome thoughts and emotions. If you feel happy amid a strife-ridden moment, do not hesitate to indulge in happiness. Celebrate the minor achievements to motivate you toward the bigger goals.

Make a Daily Goal

Decide daily to be grateful for someone or something. If you woke up and went for a twenty-minute run, choose to be thankful for that fete. Being deliberate about gratitude forces us to be more receptive to all the things in life that we, in our ignorance, fail to be thankful for. Writing down your daily gratitude goals helps you assess your improvement for the week and perhaps carry forward that emotion for the better part of the coming week.

Find a Gratitude Buddy

Find a companion to help you discuss what you are grateful for daily. It may be a friend, family member, or even a support group. You may open up to one another to fully express thankfulness.

Reduce Your Complaints

It is necessary to give complaints because it is valuable feedback; however, remain mindful of why and how often you complain. Giving a compliment for every complaint is a brilliant way to keep the scales balanced. Like every other exercise, note down every complaint and compliment you make, and in the evening, assess your day. This exercise will help keep you be attuned to your mental health.

Act of Kindness

If you have had someone you like besides your friends and family, maybe your professor or doctor, or the local fire department, write a thank you note expressing their value in the community. These people may not necessarily receive gratitude for their services, and this is your chance to give thanks. Writing this thank-you note makes the recipient feel good and reminds the sender how incredibly fortunate you are to have them.

Gratitude Prompts

The goal of this exercise is to name three things to which you are grateful. For example, I am grateful for three colors. I am grateful for three textures; I am grateful for three sounds I hear, and so on. You can start, stop, and continue this exercise at any time. Open up your senses and emotions to get the best out of this test.

Make a Collage

A gratitude collage helps you visualize the things for which you are grateful. Perhaps take pictures of things you are thankful for, and at the end of the week, take a look at your college, paying keen attention to how you feel about it. The more you practice this exercise, the more you will notice what you are grateful for.

Extensive research conducted with a group suffering from depression showed that those who practiced gratitude exercises improved faster. Gratitude is said to build emotional resilience. Meditation helps us focus our minds toward the people and things to whom we are truly grateful. Many Buddhist monks start their days and gatherings with a gratitude meditation. These meditation exercises are quick to learn and available online.

It is, however, noteworthy to say that gratitude is not an instant healer. It will not forever vanish your mental anguish and emotional strife. Therefore, do not expect a miracle. These exercises work in reminding us to accept reality and highlight the positive aspects of said reality. Gratitude exercises are a way of expressing positive thoughts towards ourselves and the world around us.

Gratitude can change your personality. Recovering from trauma can be a daunting experience because the mind undergoes reconstruction from the demolition it has continuously endured. During this reconstruction, you rediscover yourself in a new light. You may no longer go back to your previous life but, instead, be reborn into a different one where you are more aware of the many small miracles of life and are grateful for them. You may find yourself to be less materialistic while you had initially been very vain. You might become more spiritual, while initially, the notion of an eternal presence seemed far-fetched.

Daily practice of gratitude exercises helps you keep your vibration high. It is the most obvious yet overlooked technique to get what you want. There is no limit to how grateful you can be in one day. For example, if your goal is to be happy, instead of thinking about how strenuous your life is at the moment or how depressed you have been lately, focus on being appreciative of the experiences you have had and a daily renewed opportunity at life. Harness the power of gratitude to realize your desires.

Chapter 7 - Thriving Mode

Narcissistic abuse is emotional or psychological abuse directed by a narcissist on another person. Primarily, it focuses on psychological and emotional abuse, but there are other forms of narcissistic abuse, such as sexual, physical, and financial. What causes this disorder is not known but could be triggered by environmental factors, genetics, and neurobiology.

To recover from narcissistic abuse, understanding which form of narcissistic abuse exhibits and its effects is critical. Narcissistic abuse comes in the form of obsession with your mistakes, ignoring narcissist's actions, feeling worthless, devaluing your contributions, disconnection from your own needs and wants, idealizing the narcissist, and obsession with making the narcissist happy, among many others.

Even once you realize the effects, it's not easy to overcome this situation since most people don't know what to do. But it is crucial that one gets out to rediscover a sense of self and take control of their life. Below is a compilation of ways one can use to overcome the effects of narcissistic abuse and get their life back:

Set Boundaries

There is a common saying, out of sight, out of mind. When you see someone, who reminds you of something, it will be difficult to move on or disrupt the healing process. Therefore, it's the best way of overcoming narcissistic abuse if you can physically getaway. Any memory of the past with the narcissist will trigger the pain and slow down the recovery process. You may even want to consider blocking them on your phone, email, and any other ways of interactions like social media. Also, do not stalk their profiles.

Let's say it's not possible for you to physically get yourself out of their environment, possibly because of your work or other genuine reasons; there is still a technique you can employ which doesn't involve you not seeing or being close to the narcissist. This technique is called "grey rock." How this works is that while you interact with them, you remain mentally and emotionally disengaged, and by doing this, it gives them nothing to feed on. Although you might be hurting inside, do not let it show. Once you are in a place where you are alone, you can do whatever brings you relief. Screams, cry, and cuss comes to my mind; a pretty good idea, right?

A different way you can set a boundary is by practicing how to use the word NO. You do not want to be agreeing to everything. Other people must notice your stand when it comes to some matters. This will help hugely, not only by making others give you their respect but also will help you to build true confidence and self-respect. The boundary should function as a cell wall. A cell wall keeps the important nutrients in and excretes the toxic substances. Be very selective of who you let in.

It should be clear that the bottom line of setting these boundaries is a way of taking care of yourself. Limits make others aware of what to expect and definitely what to expect from them on how they treat us. When we communicate our boundaries, it's very natural for people to respect them. However, some will do all they can to resist our efforts. They may ignore, blame, and try to manipulate, or even physically hurt us. If this kind of setback occurs, you may want to re-evaluate the boundaries that are not being respected, consider other options, and take action.

Be Assertive

To overcome the abuse of the narcissist, you may not want to be aggressive or passive. One way to be assertive is by learning to use temporary reactions to handle verbal abuses. For example, "I'll do it my way." Being passive, like ignoring conflict and anger, empower the narcissist. Narcissists see this as a weakness and a chance to gain more control and power over you.

A narcissist hardly takes into account any of their evil and illegal actions. They deny the mistake and blame you for it, with no remorse, and have extreme gratification in causing pain and suffering to others. Their goal is to destroy and cause suffering and pain. The intention is to gain more control over you and continue to increase domination while developing dependency, shame, and doubt in you. When you understand this, it gives you more power to overcome the abuse.

A narcissist is a bully and will make you feel responsible for his behaviors. Do not blame yourself for anything; you have nothing to do with the abuse. Therefore, never feel any guilt because his expectations can never be met no matter how hard you try. He derives the abuse from his insecurities, and you are only accountable for how you respond. For example, you may not want to react by rationalizing, denying, or excuse his abuse. It is a lie to believe that he will improve or stop the behaviors in the future.

All the behaviors of a narcissist call for you to react assertively to put him in his corner. For example, learn more about narcissism and share the information with him. Explain his conduct, reasons, and perhaps the motivations for different behaviors. You have to plan well for how and when to do this and communicate without being emotional. Another way is facing the abuse with pure confidence because your self-esteem will get destroyed if you allow the abuse. Stand your ground and remain calm as you speak up for yourself.

Know Your Rights

Knowing your rights is very important. When you are aware of your rights, you feel entitled to something and that people must respect it. You command respect from people and let them know that you expect them to treat you in a particular manner. These rights may include: The right to be respected, do not be forced to have sex when you decline, a right to privacy, a right to opinions and feelings.

When exposed to abuse for a long time, their self-esteem will slowly diminish, and self-confidence risks being destroyed. An individual who has been involved in long-term abuse and has suffered from low self-esteem and low self-confidence will need to re-establish themselves, below are ways on how to gain self-confidence:

- Make one list of your strengths and another list of your achievements. You can get your close and supportive friend or caring relative to help you create these two lists. After that, you keep these lists in a safe place where you can read them through every morning as you wake up to a new day.

- Pay close attention to your body hygiene: Take a shower, trim your nails, and shave, brush your hair, and so on.

- Wear smart clothes that make you feel nice about yourself. Ironed outfit, for example, rather than crumpled ones.

- Exercise regularly. Register membership at the gym so you can attend sessions in your spare time or simply go for morning or evening nature walks.

- Make sure you get enough natural sleep. It's best to go to bed early and wake up early in the morning rather than sleep late and wake up late in the morning.

- Make your environment conducive. For instance, make your living space comfortable, clean, and attractive.

- Do things that you love and enjoy doing. You can watch movies, listen to your favorite music playlist, ride a bike, or swim. Anything which lifts your spirit and makes you feel good and happy.

- Think positive about yourself. Despite all the challenges and problems you might be going through now, remind yourself that you are a special someone and valuable.

- Eat healthy food. Make sure you have a balanced diet in your meals and make the moments special. Switch off the TV, set your table, and enjoy your lovely meal.

- Avoid people or places that treat you badly.

Be Strategic

You need to have a strategy on how you are going to come around this abuse. Figure out what you specifically want, your limits, and the power you have in the relationship. You should keep in mind that a narcissistic person is highly defensive. There are several strategies you can employ for this purpose. Let's take a look at some of the strategies:

Check for Abuse

When the person is emotionally or physically abusive, this should help. If you are being abused, the first thing you should do is explore why it is hard for you to exit the relationship. It doesn't matter the cause, but the reality is the abuser is responsible for their actions.

Check Your Silence

When our self-esteem has been destroyed, we occasionally resort to being silent during an argument. However, we need to find a voice if things are to get any better. Silence is a way of coping with sadness or anger.

Check Your Anger

Anger is a form of protective measure when faced with an indifferent situation. However, we need to put it on check since they cut us off from information.

Check for Their Willingness to Change

If your partner is ready to work with you, that is a big plus to improving the relationship. The easiest way to do this is by seeking help from a therapist.

Be Aware of Manipulation

Narcissists are manipulative people, and they do whatever it takes to get what they want.

Honesty to Yourself

Probably the only reason you are still holding on is hoping for the change. But there comes a point you need to be honest to yourself and admit you have tried all you can to no avail. So move on!

Be Educated

The estimated number of individuals with narcissistic disorders, based on research, varies widely. Moreover, the insight people have about narcissistic disorder, and the features of narcissism differ a lot. You need to be aware that they exist. Hence you have to inform yourself on how to recognize them. It is because of their charming behavior, which they use to conceal their narcissistic behaviors, which most people find hard to see or realize initially. This is because they do not know what to look for and how these narcissistic behaviors negatively impact their lives.

There is a lot of good information out there. Therefore, you should read as much as possible, inform yourself about this disorder, and find which insights connect well with how you are feeling.

There is also research that shows narcissists have got neurological deficits that affect interpersonal reactions. The best way to perhaps help yourself here is to educate the narcissist like a child. Find a way to explain how their behaviors impact negatively on others. Provide encouragement and incentives for different behavior. You may have to plan how you are going to communicate this without being emotional.

Confront Abuse Effectively

This is a crucial step to take. It is one way to salvage your self-esteem and confidence. Allowing abuse to continue for a long time damages your self-esteem. This should not mean you pick a fight or argue with a narcissist. It is a waste of your time and energy to argue over the facts with the abuser. They do not care about the facts but are only interested in justifying their actions and being right. Verbal arguments and the exchange of words with anger can easily escalate to fights, draining and damaging you. In this way, nothing is gained; you only end up being hurt and feeling more victimized and hopeless.

Arguing is as ineffective as making threats or pleading with the abuser to understand you. For example, making threats that you can never implement may lead to retaliation. Do not make a threat you know you cannot enforce. It is more effective and easy to set boundaries that, when not respected, lead to direct consequences. Also, pleading is a sign of weakness, which abusers despise in themselves and others. This may make them react dismissively in disgust or contempt.

Confronting the abuser, therefore, must be purposeful and should only serve to show your stand. It has to be a way of speaking up for yourself, which calls for you to do it with a clear mind and calmly. You can only manage this by setting boundaries to protect your emotions, mind, and body.

Have Consequences

It is possible that after you set your boundaries, they are ignored. For this reason, it is essential to clearly communicate the consequences and invoke them accordingly. However, you also need to set healthy boundaries that are based on mutual respect. It is important to recognize violations as they are, as this will help you create boundaries where your feelings and needs are respected.

It is also important not to set boundaries that you are unwilling to keep. You can be sure the narcissist will rebel against these boundaries and test how far you can go. You need to make sure that every broken boundary is followed up with the consequence specified. If you fail to do this, you are sending a message that you are not keen on these boundaries, and therefore you will not be taken seriously. It is really up to you to stand tall for this to be successful as the narcissist will attempt to manipulate you since they are threatened by you trying to take control of your life because they are used to being the one in power and calling the shots.

Having consequences is, therefore, without debate very useful and helpful in trying to cope with the abuse of the narcissist as long as you stand firm to the set boundaries and specified consequences. The consequences, for example, may inform you to take necessary action, such as getting out of the relationship with the narcissist as a result of a broken set of boundaries. This means it would have eventually helped you convince yourself that it's the best call to leave for your health and safety.

Get Support and Purpose Elsewhere

Support is necessary if you are to respond effectively to abuse. Without support, it is easy to languish in self-doubt and eventually succumb to narcissist's abusive disinformation. Support is essential as you may get pushback and a rebellion when you stand up against the abuse. You will need tools to defend and protect yourself and help lift your self-worth, which will alleviate how you feel whether you choose to stay or leave.

If you decide to stay in a relationship with the narcissist, you need to be honest about yourself, for example, about what you can or can't change or expect. A narcissist is not someone you can be sure things will change and start caring or valuing you. Therefore, you will have to look for emotional support elsewhere.

Spend time with individuals who will be honest with you and give you a true reflection of who you are. This will help you maintain perspective and avoid falling prey to narcissist's manipulations and distortions. In addition, they will help you validate how you feel and your thoughts. Making new friendships will also help. Narcissists will isolate you from other people to better control you and have power over you. In this case, you may want to invest more time in reviving lapsed friendships or creating new relationships.

You can also involve yourself in activities such as volunteering in your neighborhood or at work, which makes use of your abilities and talents, allowing you to make your contributions. This will help you feel good about yourself instead of looking into someone else to make you feel good.

Trust Your Intuition

This is a point where we do a reasonable post-mortem analysis, and we start to take responsibility for what will happen but disregarded it. Maybe at some early point in the relationship, you had a certain feeling in your stomach. Perhaps the things they said or the way they acted did not add up. Ask yourself what reason you had at that time to ignore your intuitive hint. It could be because you really wanted the relationship to work, or maybe their acts of "love" filled that space inside your soul, a void possibly left behind from childhood experiences.

If you never experienced true love as a child, specifically from your parents or guardians, it is normal to seek fulfillment of love now as a grown-up. However, it is a vulnerability that a narcissist may notice and use to control your life. Treat your intuition as a friend, and the more you trust and listen to it, the stronger you become and realize your self-worth.

Narcissisms are not only experienced in our love relationships; we also find them at home, places of work, our schools, and in our friendships. Therefore, we interact with these situations more often than you may think, only that maybe we don't notice them. For this reason, we learn features of narcissism to recognize when we stumble upon them and equip ourselves with tools to overcome their abuse, such as the ones highlighted above. Remember, the person with conscientiousness and sensitivity is the healthy one in the relationship, while the one with a feeling of entitlement and treats another person with disrespect is normally emotionally unhealthy.

Narcissists' central play is to destroy your confidence and self-esteem. They do this by revoking our emotions, which exposes our vulnerability. It is, therefore, helpful not to show our emotions when interacting with them as they use opportunities like this to get into us and manipulate us. Building your self-confidence will help shield you from these abuses. Refer to the ways above on how to build or re-establish your self-confidence.

Chapter 8 - Getting into a New Relationship

You might be well equipped mentally and emotionally to recognize the apparent warnings that you are starting a toxic relationship with a narcissist. But unfortunately, so many people are unaware of these red flags and will find themselves quickly attracted to these toxic people.

The good news is that a narcissistic relationship will eventually end. Narcissists tend to tire of their victims once they exploit them of their support and resources, such as money or care. They will then leave your life without as much warning, just like the way they entered.

The breakup will leave you devastated, but with time, you will appreciate their absence in your life. Once you heal from the breakup, you need to focus on moving on with your life. Here are some of the signs that will help you know that you are finally over a narcissistic relationship and ready to date again.

Signs You Are Ready for a New Relationship
You Don't Think About Them Anymore

Once you stop thinking and caring about your last love, it is an excellent sign that you are finally over them. At the initial stages of your breakup, you will be preoccupied with them, and you might be tempted to reach out for a reunion. However, you gain a new perspective with time, and you will find no reason to pay any attention to them.

Besides, once you get them out of your mind, it could mean you can comfortably meet them or hear about them through your mutual friends without having those past feelings rushing back. You find yourself not caring about them anymore.

You Have No Hatred for Them

Any relationship breakup usually comes with many conflicting emotions, especially if you break up with a narcissist. You may have intense hatred towards them, especially whenever you remember all the wrong things they did to hurt you. At times, however, you find yourself yearning to let them back into your life. All these conflicting feelings can be confusing, and you might be in a dilemma of whether to move on or go back to them. Relationship experts advise you take some time off any relationship until you have dealt conclusively with these conflicting emotions. The day you realize you don't hate your former partner anymore is the day you are entirely free. You can then move on with your life.

When You Can Open up Freely

In most cases, you may find it challenging to open up about your abusive past relationships. It could be because you are afraid of the shame and stigma that can come from such revelations. However, it is a good idea to open up to someone you trust about your past; this is an essential step in healing. When you find yourself ready to open up about your past abusive relationship, it could be a great sign that you are finally ready to move on.

Besides, opening up could mean more than just telling a close friend. Where stalking or domestic abuse is involved, it is safe for you to engage the authorities. Although you may feel you are betraying your ex, submitting a police report for your safety is good. When you realize speaking up about your abuse is the right thing to do and you no longer feel bad or guilty about it, then you know you are finally free. If you can successfully do this, then it means you are entirely free from your past relationship, and you are now ready to date again.

You Don't Stalk Them Anymore

After any break up you may be tempted to stalk your ex, primarily through social media. The temptation to find out what they are up to can be particularly overwhelming. Curiosity can never harm you, but if you find yourself curious about your narcissist ex's daily activities, then there is a cause to worry.

A narcissist can take advantage of your curious nature to pretend to be sad or anxious and suffer, knowing that you monitor their lives too well; this is how they will hook you and make you feel responsible for their emotions. But if you no longer worry about what they are up to or who they hang out with, then it is a good sign that finally, you are over them, and you are now ready to move on with your life.

You Don't Feel Wrong About Your past Experiences

You may always be tempted to judge yourself harshly for failing to see through the lies of your narcissistic ex. You may regret ignoring the apparent warnings that could have quickly helped you know you were in an abusive relationship. Still, you may be bitter at yourself for being so dumb and not running away from your abuser. All these blames are signs that you are not entirely healed, and you may not be ready for a new relationship.

Narcissists are skillful at manipulating others, and they mainly target successful and confident people to boost their image. It is no use blaming yourself for their actions.

Once you no longer feel dumb and doubtful about your critical thinking skills, then it is time you go out on a date with someone else.

You Have No Fear of Falling for a Similar Person Again

The first initial days after your breakup may make you so fearful of meeting new people. You may end up being too vigilant and always looking out so as not to meet another person who will treat you as badly as your ex.

Stopping the unnecessary caution in every person you meet is an excellent sign that you are ready to move on, meaning you can freely interact with other people without the nagging thought that they may possess the same qualities as your ex.

When you go on dates with a new guy and realize that your mind is free from any negative emotions associated with your narcissist ex, it is a good sign that you are finally over him and can now settle with someone else.

You Take Care of Yourself

Narcissist abuse can wreak havoc on you, both physically and emotionally. Going through such an experience could mean you are so stressed that you failed to take good care of yourself. As a result, you might have lost or put on too much weight. You may also have ignored the good beneficial routines that could keep you fit and healthy such as regular workouts and eating healthy food. This will result in your body responding to the negative changes, and you may have a break out of acne or even complicated diseases such as heart attacks and diabetes. As a result of stress, you may end up looking old, sad, haggard, thin, or fat.

However, once you are out of the toxic environment, you will find yourself taking good care of your body again. You may start going to the gym again. You are also more aware of the kind of food you consume, and you make a conscious effort to choose healthy food over unhealthy ones. Your body gets more robust, and your physical appearance is much improved. This could be a great sign that you are over your abusive relationship and ready to start all over again.

You Are Ready to Take the Risk Again

It is often said that great love and great achievements involve some significant risks. You may experience some nervousness at the thought of dating, especially after a breakup from an abusive relationship; this, however, is a normal feeling. But if you are convinced that your next relationship might not work out or may end up becoming an exact copy of the last one, then you probably need more time for yourself to heal fully.

The truth is all relationships carry with them some element of risk. The day you find inner strength and have come up with a solid foundation of independence, it is an excellent sign that you are ready to move on.

If you are unsure whether to on or not, then wait for a while before you make that move. Whenever you are in doubt, it is advisable to talk to someone you trust; this could be your closest friend or your counselor. But once you have cleared all your fears and doubts, it is a great moment for you to meet new people.

You Genuinely Want to Start a New Relationship

An additional sign that you are ready for a new relationship after a narcissist relationship is that you know within yourself that you genuinely want to start one. However, if you only desire to create a new relationship because you are under a lot of pressure or feel inadequate and lonely, then it is advisable not to start one. The relationship may end up being so unfulfilling and empty.

If you want to avoid further hurts, then choose to wait for that special someone who truly complements you and makes you feel happy and complete again.

However, finding this ideal person may require a lot of time and patience on your part. Once you truly feel you want to start a new relationship for the right reasons, then it is time you find that unique person whom you truly connect with and want as a partner.

Redefining Sexy After a Narcissistic Relationship

You may have encountered several pictures of what society perceives as attractive people in magazines or TV commercials. But have you ever paused to consider the meaning of being sexy? Could it be that someone somewhere is setting specific standards to the rest of us on what sexiness and attractiveness entails?

After coming through an abusive relationship, it is normal for you to be obsessed with being sexy and attractive once again. However, you should be more careful about how you go about this because sexy doesn't always mean safe. Some men may take advantage of your vulnerability and low self-esteem under the wrong assumption that you will feel grateful that any man would be attracted to you.

Besides, you should know that being sexy and attractive goes beyond the looks and all that makes up the "aura." There is an incredibly sexy and attractive person inside you who is screaming to be let out. Here is how you can redefine sexiness in your unique world and make the whole world have more than a precursory glance at you.

Don't Think You Are Unattractive; Make Yourself Attractive Instead

Learn to develop the right attitude about your attractiveness; this is an essential step in redefining your sexiness once again. If you think of yourself as attractive, then others will follow suit and find you attractive also. The change will happen at that moment; you make a conscious decision of thinking and making yourself beautiful.

Don't Let Your Past Relationship Affect Your Current Life

You kill your sexiness with fear if you carry the baggage of your past failed relationship into your present life. The pain and heartbreak you suffered in the past belong to the past. You need to deal with them conclusively for you to move into a new life of happiness. You need to learn from where you have been and be determined to emotionally make your current life better. Dealing with your past decisively builds up your confidence and makes you charming both to yourself and your friends.

Find Your Confidence

No one is as attractive and sexy as an overly confident person. You need to believe in yourself, get to know who you are. Once you master this, you will go about your daily business, exuding attractiveness to those around you. You possess an aura of mystery and send the message that you are an exciting person. If you successfully build your confidence level, most people will find you very attractive and want to be associated with you; this is one great way of making friends.

Dress Well and Give Yourself a Treat

Your choice of clothing can significantly enhance your physical features. You have to find out what clothes and colors fit you the best. Determine which clothes make you look incredible and attractive.
When you dress sharply, you tend to be more confident and attractive. Once you have dressed up, take yourself out for a date, preferably to an expensive restaurant that fits your class and status. Be comfortable with dining alone, and this will send attractive vibes to anyone watching you.

Maintain the Right Posture

One of the most attractive things in a man is his posture. Your posture and the way you generally present yourself sends a subtle message to the whole world on who you indeed are. Make intentional eye contact with people around you. Give out random smiles and stand tall, shoulders relaxed.

Learn to practice standing tall to communicate confidence in your brain, which will trigger your feelings to feel the same.

Learn the Skills of a Good Romance

Romance is not as complicated as many people think. It could be as simple as looking at your partner's eyes to find out what is going on inside them. Romance can be the choice of the words you use when communicating with your partner during the day or at night, either through word of mouth or texts and calls. When you take your time to go into the depths of your heart and select the right words to say to your lover, it can create a natural feeling of romance. Once you master the art of romance, you end up being the most romantic man or woman around, and many find passionate people to be lovely.

Love Yourself and Your Life

You need to find what goes on inside you and your heart. You are a precious person who has so much to offer to oneself and the rest of the world. Create a great interest in your life, which motivates you to keep waking up every morning. Develop a sense of purpose that prompts you to find out why you exist and how you can bring a difference to your world.

Learn to take full control of your life to spend your time doing the things that make you happy and which can positively impact the lives of others. Learn to listen to your inner feelings and strive to satisfy your desires and drives. Once you learn to love yourself and your life, you will make yourself an incredibly attractive and sexy person.

How to Become Your Own Source of Happiness

They say you are responsible for your satisfaction, and the truth of this statement cannot be disputed. Your satisfaction is actually within your control. You should avoid letting external forces control your happiness. Instead, use the following tips to create your happiness:

Make Yourself a Priority

You should show yourself some real love by prioritizing what makes you happy; this shouldn't be random but should be a routine practice that you do regularly each day. Get out and give yourself a treat for no reason once in a while. Put on your favorite music and dance to it. Go for a pedicure and manicure. You should also go for a shopping day and get yourself that fancy expensive dress you dreamed of. Engage in activities that make you fulfilled, refreshed, and recharges your battery to make you happy.

Do the Little Things You Love More Often

You don't have to do fancy stuff for you to be happy. Sometimes you find happiness in the small things you do. It could be a sip from your favorite coffee brand or that delicious meal, which puts a cheer on your face. It could be watching your favorite program or movie. Or it could be that yoga exercises which you find so relaxing and therapeutic. Find those little things that make you happy and do them more.

Challenge Yourself by Doing Something New

You need to break your monotonous, boring routines and, once in a while, do something new; this will give you happiness and renew your energy. Try something new which you have never tried before. It could be that hike across the hill or sky diving. Go for activities that set off your adrenaline.

Get Enough Sleep

Sleep is vital in improving your mood, happiness, and self-control. Sleep enables your brain to recharge and get rid of toxic by-products of the healthy brain neural function. Getting enough sleep ensures you wake up feeling energized, focused, and stress-free.

Do the Workouts

Exercises improve your mood and contribute immensely to your happiness. Studies show that peoples who engage in regular workouts are far happier, productive, and successful in achieving their life goals. Exercise also helps to limit impulsivity.

How to Stay Single and Blessed

You may be struggling to remain comfortable after a breakup. However, happiness is not necessarily tied to your soulmate. It is possible to be single and happy. You need to learn how to be happy without depending on the status of your relationship. The following tips will help you to be alone and happy.

Learn to Do Things on Your Own

Most people are afraid of carrying out their normal activities on their own. You need to learn to go shopping by yourself. Go out for movies or dinner alone. Learn to enjoy your life by yourself. Your happiness is your personal choice, and it is not through being attached to someone else.

Develop Other Relationships

You need to foster other meaningful relationships with family or friends. It is not a condition for you to be romantically involved to be happy. Family and friends can be a great source of support and happiness. Create more time for them because they offer the most exceptional support whenever you face life's challenges.

Meet New People

You need to cultivate the necessary skills that enable you to meet up with new people without necessarily having a romantic date. Talk to other people but, more importantly, listen to what they have to say on a wide range of issues. You need to step out of your comfort zone and intentionally set up meetings with new people.

Treat Yourself

While you are single, you should maintain a positive self-image. Go out shopping and get yourself new outfits. Get a fresh pedicure or a manicure, spend time in a spa, or get yourself that excellent massage. Ensure you do beautiful things to yourself more frequently. You are a wonderful individual who deserves the best.

Maintain a Supportive, Positive Company

Don't spend too much time alone. Spend more time with the people who make you happy. Join a club if necessary. Moreover, ensure you are in the right company of people who resonates with some positive energy. Get support from people you can trust and who are not judgmental about your single status.

Conclusion

Thank you for reading *Narcissistic Abuse Healing Guide: Follow the Ultimate Narcissists Recovery Guide, Heal and Move on From an Emotional Abusive Relationship! Recover From Narcissism or Narcissist Personality Disorder! We hope the information provided* you and your loved ones with all the tools you need to overcome any instances of narcissistic abuse. By finishing this book, you will be able to possess the mastery you seek in dealing with any narcissists around you and how to feel better even after suffering as a narcissistic victim.

We have gone through the success stories of narcissistic abuse and the understanding of narcissistic personality disorder. This book has offered easy-to-use but very powerful and effective techniques for tackling any signs of narcissistic abuse. You are now familiar with the concept of pseudo personality. You have further learned about the strategies necessary for dealing with pseudo personality, including how you can acknowledge that you have a pseudo personality.

For this book to work for you, you must encompass all the advice and techniques you have read. It may not be in the order that it has been listed in this book, but you must use all of them for maximum benefits. You are now aware that you must know and decide to overcome any memory challenges, regardless of the cause. And the next thing you would want to do is put in a request for what you want.

This book will have provided you with the tools to start over a life full of activeness, awareness, and memorization of important experiences in life.

Finally, if you found this book useful in any way, an honest review is always appreciated!

www.ingramcontent.com/pod-product-compliance
Lightning Source LLC
Chambersburg PA
CBHW060406080526
44583CB00012B/489